The Ocean is Calling

ASHLEY BUGGE

the ocean
is calling

A True Story

of Love and Loss

by the Sea

NEW YORK

LONDON • NASHVILLE • MELBOURNE • VANCOUVER

The Ocean is Calling

A True Story of Love and Loss by the Sea

Published in New York, New York, by Morgan James Publishing. Morgan James is a trademark of Morgan James, LLC. www.MorganJamesPublishing.com

Proudly distributed by Ingram Publisher Services.

ISBN 9781631958663 paperback
ISBN 9781631958670 ebook
Library of Congress Control Number:
2022933210

Cover Design by:
Megan Dillon
megan@creativeninjadesigns.com

Interior Design by:
Christopher Kirk
www.GFSstudio.com

Morgan James is a proud partner of Habitat for Humanity Peninsula and Greater Williamsburg. Partners in building since 2006.

Get involved today! Visit MorganJamesPublishing.com/giving-back

Dedication

For Isabel, Hudson, and Adeline. You are too young to remember many of these stories, but I hope they fill your mind with wonder and excitement as you grow older and read them. You were born explorers and I am humbled every day by your zest and excitement for life. You three are hands down my greatest adventure. I love you.

To Brian, my love. Thank you for the time we had together and for the love we shared which has made this journey without you so unbearably hard. I think of you every day and in every way. The kids are growing into little explorers just like their dadda, and you'd be so proud and excited about the love they have for the ocean and all of its creatures. We love you and we miss you, darling. A Hui Hou.

Table of Contents

Acknowledgment

Nikki. I could spend pages of this book trying to express my gratitude toward you and yet it will never be enough. This book is dedicated to you. My sister, my friend, my confidant, my caretaker. You held my hand through it all and I am forever grateful to your brother for bringing you into my life. To Uncle Aaron, Elliot, and Kaius thank you for opening your heart and your home to us when we needed it most and for bearing with us during those dark days on East Copper Ridge.

Grandma Kasey and Kay. Thank you for saying yes. This trip saved me in ways you can't imagine, and I could not have done it without you. Through the many ups and downs, lost luggage, skinned knees, itinerary changes, and more laughter and tears than any of us thought possible, you were there for it all. Thank you for believing in me and giving my family these memories. Malta Forever!

Mama T and Gpa. For making your house a home and for always making me feel like a daughter without the "in-law" part. For reindeer games and book launch parties, for laughter and shared tears. You are my family and I love you. To Ma & Dad, Zack, Kellie, Benny, Jenn. Thank you for dropping everything to fly to a rock in the middle of the ocean when I needed you most. For holding my hand and wiping my tears, for remembering and loving Brian. The kids and I are lucky to call you our family.

To Aunt Jess. For staying with me when I really needed you. For continuing to show up and loving on these kids—even with the never-ending Amtrak schedule changes. For the inside jokes & movie quotes, the body-slams and monster jam rallies, trips to Walgreens and hermit-crab races, you really are one-in-a-million and I'm forever grateful for your friendship, sis.

To Brunella. This story wouldn't have been told without your help. I'm humbled and grateful to have met you and know there is so much more ahead for both of us.

To Adrian, Eric, Jaime, Josh, Chris, Gary, Ryan P., Courtney, and the rest of the year-one dive team. You are the reason I feel at peace back in the water, and that is a gift you'll never understand the value of. Thank you for trusting me. It's been an honor to dive with you all.

To NeeNee, Auntie Linda & Uncle Robert, Jenn Blankenbaker, Uncle Bert & Aunt Lindsay, Meesh & the PHS band nerd crew, Chananny, Uncle Mike, Brae, The Martin Fam, Jason Bad

Guy, Alissa Evans & fam, Aunt Sharon, Gareth, David C., and our Hawaiian Ohana. It has taken the love, support, and guidance of each of you to get the kids and I to where we are today. Each of you have played such a pivotal role in our lives these last few years and we couldn't have done this without you. Here's to many more shared memories ahead.

To Morgan James Publishing. For believing in the power of this story and the platform to share it.

To all of those who have read 'Always Coming Back Home' and/or 'A Hui Hou: Until We Meet Again.' Thank you for your unwavering support, and for joining the kids and I on this incredible journey these last few years. This is for you.

Chapter One

The six of us landed in Anker, Norway on a gorgeous summer morning. Three adults, three children, and a cool breeze which traveled across the Bygdøy Peninsula until it danced over our faces like an invisible kiss… there and then gone in an instant. I closed my eyes and moved my face upward to the sun to take it all in. We were finally here. This had taken a full year of planning, and after what we had all just gone through, it was finally sinking in; we'd made it. Even the air smelled different than it did in Hawaii, where we'd lived since my husband's last assignment with the Navy.

My husband. Brian James Bugge. The man whose fascination with the ocean would take us through this story and beyond, simultaneously weaving the absolute best and worst days of my life into a series of minutes, moments, and memories.

As a naval officer working on submarines, he had been sent to foreign ports around the world, often calling home with vivid descriptions of where he was staying and what things looked like, sometimes offering an idea of what things cost. "Babe, things in Dubai are so expensive! Japan is so clean and everyone is so friendly! The diving in Guam is world-class, I've never experienced anything like it!"

A born explorer, he had chosen this career in the Navy because of the travel and adventure it was sure to offer him, and he looked forward to getting to explore new parts of the world while getting paid to do it. Taiwan, Indonesia, Djibouti…he had traveled all over, each place offering something unique and special, typically more exciting and adventure-packed than the previous. He'd bring home tokens of his travels; gifts for me and the kids, mugs for the cupboard, framed photos or wooden carvings, always with stories of who he bought them from and the meaning behind each item. He had traveled so much, but was always sure to say that no place compared to home; home was his favorite place on earth. Until he went to Norway. Norway was special. Norway stuck. Norway quickly became one of Brian's favorite work trips, falling more in love with it each passing visit; the green of the trees, the blue of the oceans, and the discovery of a new land full of adventure waiting to be had. "Babe," he called from halfway across the world on his first visit, breathless with excitement, "you HAVE to go with me the next time! Can you get the time off work? I promise you'll love it. Wait until you see the color of the water! Let's take a few extra days so we can dive too! "

Brian spoke fondly of Norway to anyone who would listen, reminiscing about visiting the lands of his ancestors, wanting to bring his own family here to see where his last name comes from. "You don't understand, it's just *so* beautiful! It's like the Oregon coast, but better!" He was smitten with this country, painted a gorgeous image of it in my own mind, and his excitement was infectious. We often used his work travels as an excuse for family vacations, being that the military paid for his plane ticket and hotel room so the kids and I had minimal expenses to meet him wherever he was in the world. Brian was really excited about Norway, and I was excited too.

I envisioned verdant mountain ranges and deep, grayish-blue seas and bays that, along with the fjords, created almost a lava lamp of undulating movement around the stillness of the land. It was my brand of adventure and he knew it. The ocean, the mountains, the outdoors, the unknown; a trip to Norway with my love couldn't come fast enough.

And so we planned.

But I never planned for my first trip to Norway to *not* include Brian.

"Mrs. Bugge? I'm calling from the dive shop, there's been an accident involving your husband, where are you right now? Are you home? Do you have your children with you? We're coming to get you."

May 20, 2018. A date etched in infamy. A date that forever changed me. A date that changed my family, my future, and the way I live my life. Yet I remember very little about the day itself or the days following. The flashbacks I have are blurred, memories scattered, with only a few distinct moments that appear when I close my eyes.

Didn't make it.

        Quiet Room.

So Sorry.

        Call Someone.

Family.

        Dead.

Tried.

        Calm Down.

Dead.

A few distinct smells and sounds pull me back to that day. The smell of the ocean all at once replaced by the antiseptic smell of the hospital. The sounds of crashing waves giving way to complete silence then to an incessant ringing in my ears. Images I wished I never had to re-see, the ones that stick with you and are impossible to forget. *A panicked pregnant woman collapsing in the hallway of the ER. A doctor with tears in her eyes saying, "I'm sorry." A woman with blonde curly hair suddenly standing over me. Does she know Brian? Cold tile floor. Weightlessness. Am I being carried? "Your babies need you." Who's talking? Who are these people? Wake up, Ashley. Wait, I'm that pregnant woman. What happened? Why am I on the floor? What's going on? Where's Brian?*

Brian. The love of my life. The brown-haired man with piercing blue eyes I had watched walk out the door of our home only hours earlier. Brian. My husband. The man I met when we were just twenty years old and grew up going to punk rock shows together with our young friends; goofy, careless, full of excitement for all that was ahead. The shy and sweet, yet adventurous boy I wasn't ready for at such a young age, but who I fell head over heels with nine years later when our paths crossed again. Brian. My soulmate. The man I married on a crisp November day at the Oregon coast, in the very spot he first told me, "I love you" who I was living my happily-ever-after with. Brian James. Sailor, explorer, naval officer, diver. The father to our two children, Isabel (Izzy) born in 2014, and Hudson born in 2016, as well as soon-to-be-born Adeline, the daughter we had recently found out we were pregnant with and who would be joining our family in August 2018. My love, Brian.

Most of the gaps have been filled by stories of friends and family members who rushed to my side as soon as they learned of his tragic drowning. Many of them had been alerted by Linda who I managed to call on my way to the emergency room when all I knew was that Brian had been involved in a scuba diving accident and I needed to get there. Quickly. Linda was a mother figure to me, and despite the fact I had been her manager at the bank we both worked at in Washington state, we quickly became close friends and were elated when her husband, Robert, received his own orders with the Air Force to relocate his family to Oahu where Brian, Izzy, Hudson and I had just moved. Linda and Robert had become dear friends to Brian and I over the years and had taken on the role of surrogate grandparents to our children, often accompanying us on our family beach days or to browse the fruit and veggie stands at the *Kaka'ako* farmers market, as Linda had done that very day prior. On a rock in the middle of the ocean, far away from any of our family and loved ones, Linda and Robert were the closest thing I had to family.

"Linda, Brian's been in an accident!! Linda, help!" I cried into the phone. Without any questions and without any answers, Linda rushed to the hospital to be with me as I received the news that I wasn't prepared to hear: Brian James Bugge, thirty-five years old with that irresistible dimple on his left cheek, the love of my life, my partner in crime, the man I had promised to love all the days of his life, was gone. *Gone.*

***

> *"I promise to love, honor and cherish you, until death do us part."* *He said to me on our wedding day; a cold November morning in Manzanita, Oregon. We stood barefoot on the course pale sand, holding hands and sneaking kisses as our wedding officiant had us repeat after her. "I do. I do!" We were married! He grabbed me by the waist, kissed my lips, and whispered, "I love you, wife."*

***

Linda wasn't with us on our wedding day, but she had been with us for many other relationship milestones. A military spouse herself, she held my hand and let me cry on her shoulder every time Brian was sent out for deployment on the submarines he'd loved working on for the past fourteen years. She'd held my hair back as I experienced pregnancy morning sickness in the waste-paper basket of the bank where we worked, and she'd squeezed me tightly when Brian had received orders from the Navy to report to Hawaii for his next assignment, meaning the Navy would be moving us from our home state of Washington. With her Guamanian heritage, she had deep brown hair, always-tanned skin and the warmest smile. Linda was a once-in-a-lifetime kind of friend, and now here she was to hold my hand through another one of life's big milestones.

Linda found me in the room with Brian—the quiet room, as the hospital staff referred to it—huddled over him, trying to warm him up and bring him back to me. She did her best to console me as she rubbed my back, wiped the tears from my eyes, held a bag to my mouth as I got sick and answered questions from the hospital staff and investigators on my behalf. She never left my side. Linda had been my friend through all of the stages of my relationship with Brian; as we got engaged, then married, had babies, moved to Hawaii, and now she was there during this final stage as she watched me say goodbye to him.

Linda stood next to me in that quiet room, reminding me to breathe, reminding me that I had Brian's and my third baby in my belly and that I needed to find a way to calm down. As the hospital staff came and left the quiet room, pulling Linda outside to talk, she'd come back in and remind me that Isabel and Hudson were still waiting in the car and needed me, telling me we'd need to leave soon. *Isabel and Hudson, outside in the car, one and three years old. I have to tell them their dad is dead? I can't. This isn't real.* I couldn't fathom it. I wasn't ready to face the reality. I wasn't ready to say the words. Linda disappeared again and when she returned, looked at me and with tears in her eyes and said it was time to go. I knew I had to check on my children. They were outside in the car with the man from the dive shop who had called me a few hours earlier to say, "Mrs. Bugge, there's been an accident on your husband's dive boat." The same man who had driven to my house moments after that call, picked us all up and raced through the streets of Honolulu to the emergency room. The same man who watched me run across that emergency room parking lot six months into my latest pregnancy, unsure and terrified of what I was about to find inside. I knew him only by name, Brian having spoken about him from time to time as somebody he worked with at the shop. He was a stranger to me up until this moment, and yet his words during that phone call changed my entire life and who now waited outside with my young children whose entire lives were about to be changed by *my* words. I wasn't ready to leave. As agitated and in shock as I was, I knew the moment I walked out of that hospital room, I would never see Brian again...I'd never touch him, kiss him, hold him...I wasn't ready for our love story to be over. *This couldn't be it for us.*

I couldn't let go. I wouldn't let go. I held on to his cold body as tight as I could, convinced this was a terrible dream and I'd be waking up soon. Even as I watched Brian's dive team come in to say their goodbyes, friends who had been in the water with him that morning and now sported bloodshot eyes, damp, disheveled hair and scruffy faces—such vivid details that usually come in a dream, I was convinced this wasn't real life.

"I've wanted to learn to scuba dive since I was thirteen years old!" Brian had hold me. "I used to read the books by Jacques Cousteau and dream of life under the water. We could dive and travel the world together once I'm certified! I just have one more class and dive to do before I get this certification..."

There was too much going on, too many emotions, too many people, too much to think through, when I heard the words, "Honey, is there anybody we should call?" I looked up at Linda with fear in my eyes and panic on my face at the realization that if this wasn't a dream, if this indeed was really happening, I'd have to call family members to let them know. How was I going to say *the words*? I didn't even believe it myself yet. How was I going to make anybody else believe what I was looking at? "Linda, I need to call Brian's mom. What if she wants to see him? To say goodbye? Linda, what do I say?" Before I could fully understand what I was doing, I had dialed her number and the phone was ringing.

It was a sunny Sunday afternoon in Boise, Idaho, and it was our weekend ritual to chat as a family via Facetime, to give updates on the kids and island life no matter where we were all physically located at the time. Brian had grown up with his mom, Terry, step-dad, Frank, and sister, Nikki, but had moved away when he was eighteen-years old, so he hadn't lived in close proximity to any of his family for over a decade. Raised by a single-mom until Frank joined the family, Brian had always been a mama's boy; the pride and joy of Terry's life, and no matter where he was in the world, he always made time to call home to check in with her, to provide updates of deployments and travel, to share funny stories of the kids and to get the scoop on his niece and nephew. His sister, Nikki was often present for these phone calls as well, and the warmth and closeness they all shared as a family was something that had drawn me in from the very beginning. Terry and Frank would be expecting a call from us today with a recap of our week.

Ring. Ring. Ring. "Hey sweetheart! How's my baby doing?" Brian's mother said cheerfully as she answered the phone. She was referring to baby Adeline, our third child, due to be born in a few months and whose name Brian and I had decided on only days prior. *"Oh, Terry. I..."* I started. *"Is Frank with you?"* She sounded so happy. This was going to be excruciating. She'd had no warning—there had been no warning. *"Yes honey, he's here next to me... Is everything ok?"* I could hear her put me on speaker phone. She had no expectation that this wouldn't be our normal weekend call. I hovered over Brian's lifeless form in the hospital bed next to me, her first-born and only son. *"Terry... Frank.... I..."* My husband, my best friend. Isabel, Hudson, and Adeline's dad. Their son. I willed myself to breathe. *You have to say it, Ash.* With the phone to my ear, I looked up, I looked around, and eventually I cleared my throat and looked down. I was staring at my husband, the endotracheal tube still placed in his throat—a visual representation of the efforts made to save his life, to bring him back to me—but now it was just there, attached to nothing, his tongue protruding slightly from his mouth because of its placement. *This can't be real.* I squeezed Brian's cold hand, silently willing him to squeeze it back, but instead of reassurance and comfort, I found the IV catheter which had been placed on the ambulance ride to the hospital, now dry and not connected to anything, because he was gone. *He is gone.* And now I had his mom on the phone, and I was about to tell her that her son had died. *How do I tell her? What do I say?* I didn't even believe this myself, so how was I going to make *her* believe it? This was going to be one of the worst phone calls I'd ever have to make, but the emergency room doctor had delivered the words to me, and now I needed to say them to her.

"Terry...I need to talk to you guys...I...Oh Terry...I don't know how to say this...I... There's been a terrible accident..." I said, breaking down in tears and immediately regretting it because I knew they were going to assume that something bad had happened to the baby. "Honey? Ashley? What's wrong? Ash?" I could hear the panic swell in their voices as they said my name. I took a breath, and with Linda sitting next to me, I said *the words*. It didn't sound like me, but I could feel the breath escaping my lips. "Brian was in a scuba diving accident this morning and...he...died. Terry...he died." I was lightheaded. The room spun wildly and the image of Brian in front of me slowly became fuzzy. *I'm going to be sick.* I was in a fog, but crystal clear were the next sounds emitted through the phone lines of Terry's scream. A heart-wrenching scream only made possible by the emotion of your heart tearing in half—a visceral, panicked, and desperate plea of something, or someone—severely wounded. With a single phone call, received from the middle of the ocean, Terry lost her only son. Frank lost his step-son and Nikki lost her brother. I cried. And cried. And cried. I had reached my breaking point and knew if this was real, I wouldn't survive it. Terry and Frank began asking questions to which I had no answers; I didn't know anything except that my own heart was broken, shattered beyond repair. I didn't know what to do. I became panicked, the scene in front of me suddenly becoming too real to comprehend, and I hyperventilated. Linda took the phone from my shaking hands and spoke quietly into the receiver, promising Frank and Terry to stay the night with me until they were able to get to Hawaii, and then said goodbye.

Soon after we hung up the phone, the nurse arrived, asking to see Linda again in the hallway. I continued to hover over Brian, holding his hand, kissing his cheek, running my fingers through his dark hair, slightly sticky from having been submerged in the salt water that morning. I knew what they were talking about out there, but I didn't want to hear it. *They're going to make me leave.* Linda walked back into the room with a solemn but determined look on her face as she came over to me and said, "Ash, sweetheart, we have to go now. Izzy and Hudson have been in the car for a long time and they're really upset. They need you. You need to be strong for them sweetheart." I cried even harder. I felt deep down they were using Izzy and Hudson being upset as a trick to lure me out of the room. I'd heard the hushed whispers of the nurses in the hallway inquiring about Brian being an organ donor, and he and I had discussed these wishes in detail—I knew it was what he wanted in the event we were to ever find one another in this situation—but I wasn't ready. I knew they needed his body to make this final wish come true, but I needed him more. I begged. I pleaded. I needed more time. But they couldn't give me more time, this was it and I knew it.

I took one last look at my husband. Brian James Bugge, the guy who left me love notes on our bathroom mirror in the mornings and who I couldn't wait to see after work in the evenings; the guy who had spent the summer sailing our yellow sailboat across the Pacific Ocean, the guy who had tucked our children into bed the night prior and kissed me goodbye that very morning, the guy I experienced some of life's greatest adventures with. Brian James Bugge, the love of my life. I kissed his hands, I kissed his cheek and with hot tears streaming down my face, I said goodbye. *I love you.*

Chapter Two

Linda held me by the arm and gently guided me out of the quiet room and into the Emergency Room reception area. It was the same room, and same hallway I had been standing in only an hour prior when I saw the double doors open, the doctor and security guard walking toward me with somber expressions on their faces. I had screamed then, and I was screaming now. This couldn't be happening. Not to us. We were supposed to grow old together.

"Honey," I heard Linda say, "I need you to breathe. The kids need you to be strong now."

I can't. Linda, I can't. My children. Brian's children. Our children. What was I going to say to them now? They were going to ask me, "What's the matter, Mamma? Where's Dadda?" And then? I'm just supposed to tell them their dad died? I'm just supposed to tell our babies that they'll never see him again?

No. There's no way. Hudson's one, Izzy's three. They don't even know what death or dying means. I just couldn't. The evening before, their dad had given them a bath, put them to bed, kissed and hugged them both goodnight and now he wouldn't be coming home? Ever? It was unfathomable even to me. How would I explain this to them? And yet I had to. We drove home in silence, the kids knowing something had changed, but unsure of what it was. We pulled into the driveway of our home on Bridges Street, the brown house with the beautiful birds of paradise plant in the front yard we'd moved into only eight months prior. Linda helped me carry the kids through the front door, our lopsided wooden sign reading *E Komo Mai*, welcome in Hawaiian, greeting us as we passed through its frame before sitting down on the couch.

"Dadda was in an accident this morning," I spoke softly, fighting through tears and barely able to get *the words* out. I didn't want to say it to them, but I continued on in a whisper: "He loves you guys so much, he didn't mean to, but he drank too much ocean water and he now he can't come home. Dadda is going to be diving forever." Hudson and Isabel were curled up in my lap. They looked up at me with their bright blue eyes and blond, sun-bleached hair, questioning what these words meant. The three of us sat huddled together on a single cushion of the red sectional couch we'd purchased only months prior when we'd made the move to Hawaii on Brian's military orders. We'd celebrated a single Christmas on this red couch, stockings stuffed full of toys and candy placed on either end for the kids and then Easter baskets overflowing with more of the same only a few months later. We had watched countless hours of *Blue Planet* as a family of four on this couch. Brian and I sat on this couch and discussed baby names for our third baby we'd recently found out we'd be expecting. This red couch had become a part of our home, and in essence, a part of our family these past few months. Now, only hours after receiving the devastating news that my husband had died, it was again the centerpiece of a family milestone. Isabel and Hudson shuffled in my lap, my six-month pregnant belly sticking out somewhere between their little bodies as we hugged and cried, the red couch enveloping us in a soft hug. We were devastated. Sad. Broken. Scared. The red couch caught our tears as we processed what *these words* would mean for us as a family moving forward.

We sat huddled together as Izzy attempted to process what I'd just told them. "But I don't want Dadda to dive forever, I'll miss him!" she said, her eyes filled with tears of exhaustion and incomprehensible fear. "Can he come home tomorrow? Can we visit him in the ocean?" she whispered while sobbing. "What if he gets eaten by a shark?"

I didn't know how to answer any of these questions. I had so many of my own, with nobody to ask them to, and I was just as confused and scared as my young children were. I wanted him to come home just as much as they did, and desperately willed myself to wake up from this dream, to look up and see him walk in the front door from his day of diving. "I know, kiddo, I love you so much, I'm so sorry sweetheart..." We scooted as close together as we could, scared, confused, and trying to comprehend what this meant for each of us. Izzy and Hudson both cried in my arms as I thought about what to do, where to go from here, looking up from time to time to see if this dream was over, if Brian was home yet.

***

Brian had been deployed when we found out we'd be expecting our first daughter, Izzy. We married on a Sunday, celebrated Thanksgiving on Thursday and then he flew to Bahrain to meet up with his submarine Friday. Monday morning I woke up not feeling well, drove to the neighborhood pharmacy, and four pregnancy tests later I was texting my husband across the world telling him to facetime me when he woke up. He came home from that deployment when I was six months pregnant, and a few short weeks later, he was holding his first-born child, Isabel Blakely, in his arms. I've never seen a man more proud and in his element than I did watching Brian become a dad. Two years later those feelings multiplied when we found out we'd be welcoming Hudson Belmont, a son, to our family. Brian talked endlessly about how he'd teach Hudson to sail, dive, camp and explore. He and Izzy had been extraordinarily close, but by the time Hudson joined our family, Brian was the happiest I've ever seen him. He was born to be a dad and he was living his dream with a successful career he'd worked hard for as a naval officer, a family that was able to travel with him, healthy happy kids and a supportive wife, a passport full of stamps, a life of adventure filled with sailing trips across the ocean, underwater exploration, constant travel. This was the good stuff and we knew it. We also knew we wanted to have one more child to complete our family, and after two heartbreaking miscarriages, we were both weary but ecstatic to find out we'd be having one more daughter. Adeline Makai would be joining us in August 2018 and we would spend our days on the water, teaching our kids to love and respect the ocean, but to adventure and explore every step of the way. Happiness is found in the journey, and we were on the journey of a lifetime as a family of soon-to-be-five.

***

Linda never left our sides. She slept on that red couch in our living room, cuddled Izzy and Hudson throughout the day and night, brought me glasses of water from time to time and urged me to take a sip. She made every phone call, delivering the devastating news to family and friends across the country, each dial tone and subsequent "Hello?" becoming more and more painful. She answered questions, coordinated flights, offered guidance and sympathy, and still looked after us as she processed her own grief in losing Brian. I would not have made it through the day without Linda, and in no uncertain terms, I would not have made it through the night without her there, either. She stayed with me as family began arriving the next morning; Terry and Frank, my mom and dad, my brothers and sisters, their families, Brian's sister and her family, cousins, friends, coworkers, each answer of the door more excruciating than the previous because it was further proof this was real and Brian was really gone.

At some point during the first few days, a knock on our front door startled me from my thoughts, and Linda's husband, Robert, went to answer it.

"Ash, honey. There are a couple of guys from the Navy here who need to talk to you. Is it OK to let them in?" Robert's voice was gentle, but I could hear the urgency in it. A military man himself, he knew what these men were here to say.

"OK," was all I could muster the energy to say.

Robert walked back to the door and I could hear hushed voices. When I looked up again, Robert was gone, and in his place stood three naval officers in their white dress uniforms. I gasped. *This is a scene from a movie. A book I've read. There's no way this is real life, not my life, not our life.* This memory is crystal clear…The sound of my panicking at the sight of them in my living room. The vision was too much for me to handle. It was reality slapping me in the face. I suddenly knew *why* they were there. I'd anticipated the thought of this exact moment during every single deployment, every time Brian was in a potentially dangerous situation on the submarine in far stretches of the world. I dreaded the idea of three men showing up to my house in dress whites to give me his official death notification.

"Mrs. Bugge? My deepest condolences to you and your family. I am here on behalf of the United States Navy to notify you—" I couldn't let him finish. I pulled the red couch pillow over my face. I didn't want to see these uniforms. I didn't want to hear them tell me Brian was dead. I didn't want to believe it. I found Robert's gaze through the crowd in my living room and through a fresh set of tears, asked if they could leave.

Robert spoke to them outside, asking them to change their uniforms and return when possible in "civilian clothes" to begin going through everything I'd need to know in the coming weeks and months. I'd been assigned to Nate, a casualty assistance calls officer (CACO) from Brian's navy command, who would help me with funeral preparations, sort through paperwork, benefits, and find the answers to every single question, concern, and worry I had during the process. I can't imagine a more depressing day of work than having to notify a pregnant woman with two small kids at home that her husband, his own coworker, had died...but he did, and Nate did everything in his power to make sure I knew I had not only his support, but that of the entire navy behind my family to help me through the weeks, months, and years ahead.

In the hours and days following Brian's death, I was faced with more questions and urgent decisions needing to be made than I could have ever prepared for.

"Do you want Brian to be cremated?" *Yes, I know this is what he wanted.*

"Brian is registered as an organ donor. Do you consent to the donation of his organs? *Yes.* How about bones? Tissue? Eyes and skin?" *Wait, what? Please don't ask me this. I'm going to be sick.*

"Do you still have health insurance? Can you still live in military housing?" *I don't know? Brian died on active duty, and we have military health insurance, but...what about now? We live in base housing! Where do the kids and I go? I don't know what to do. I can't go back to work like this.*

"Are you going to stay here to have the baby?" *Oh no. The baby. I'm due in two months. What do I do? Do I stay here by myself? Move off the island? I can't do this alone. Where do I go? I can't give birth in Hawaii. I can't live here. This was supposed to be our paradise. I can't bring her home to all of this sadness. Everywhere I look are memories of him, of us, of our family. But where do I go, and when?*

"I support whatever decision you make and understand if you don't want to give birth here, but I can't let you fly after you hit the thirty-two-week mark." My doctor wrote in a response to one of the messages my family had sent her office. There it was.

I was currently twenty-eight weeks pregnant with Adeline, so that gave me just under four weeks. One month to plan my husband's funeral, pack up my home, my kids, my dog, uproot our lives here, say goodbye, and start a brand-new one as a pregnant widow with two small children in tow... somewhere. *Widow.* There it was, the first time I had to say that word.

A pregnant widow? How could this be? How is this real? Unsure and incapable of processing my emotions, I started writing it all down. A place where I could work through my thoughts, worries, concerns, sadness, and share my struggles and moments of weakness during this process. Writing and publishing these thoughts forced me to be in the moment, to share my grief with others, and in a way to get it off my chest so that I could push forward. Twelve days after losing Brian, I opened my computer and bared my heart to those willing to listen.

June 1, 2018.

It's 9:00 p.m. here and I have no other word to describe how I'm feeling right now other than overwhelmed. Today was Hudson's second birthday. Two years ago, Brian held my hand as I cried in agony giving birth to this perfect little human. Brian encouraged me and pushed me and rubbed my back through every single contraction until Hudson was born. Today, looking at Hudson as fifty of my closest friends and family sang Happy Birthday to him—in a time that should be filled with so much joy—all I could think was that Brian should be standing next to me as we sing to him together. This is Brian's son and Hudson will never get to hear his dad sing Happy

Birthday to him again in his life. He'll never get those really cool presents that dads give their sons on landmark birthdays.

We celebrated Hudson's second birthday on Friday, June 1, and held Brian's funeral the next day, Saturday, June 2. Nate helped me organize the entire event, right down to designing and printing programs, selecting the music, and preparing a slideshow of photos showing smiling faces and happy times spent as a family. Brian's white officer's uniform, boots, and cover sat at the front of the chapel on display as the benches filled with his coworkers and peers, all dressed in their own uniforms out of respect for their fallen brother. Their hearts weighed heavy at the sight of the uniform, missing the man who had occupied it only days prior. Brian was so incredibly proud of his naval career, and I knew he would have been humbled to see this many people present to pay their respects to him and his service to our country.

I wore a black dress and the black *aloha* printed flip-flops we'd purchased our first week on the island, and I stayed in the back room of the chapel, clutching the brass urn containing what was left of my husband, while people filed into the chapel. Nate had driven me to the funeral home that very morning to pick ~~him~~... *it* up, and walked with me into a darkened room to see for the first time, not only the brass urn, but three small blue urns next to it, one for each of our children, containing the remains of their father. It was excruciating. I grabbed the urn and crumpled to the floor as Nate did his best to console me, handing me tissue and fighting back his own tears. *This isn't real. I can't do this. I don't want to do this.*

Now here I was, here we were, with urns in hand, waiting for Brian's funeral to begin. Somebody in a freshly tailored white uniform suddenly appeared and asked, "Mrs. Bugge, would you like me to put that up front on the table with your husband's uniform?" Sitting in the back room of the chapel, this piece of brass in my arms was all I had left of my husband, and I wasn't about to let it out of my sight or my arms. "No, thank you," I managed to reply as I hugged it tighter. "I don't feel good," I said to my sister, Jessica, seated next to me. She had known Brian as long as I had, first meeting him when she worked in Portland booking bands for shows and he'd been the singer of the metal band, Inked in Blood. She had been ecstatic when we'd first dated, disappointed when we'd broken up, and then ecstatic when we reunited in 2013 and were married. "You two are so gross, but I'm happy for you." She had been a part of Brian and I meeting and our subsequent love story, and her own heart was breaking as she sat next to me, the sights and sounds of his funeral in front of us.

"Can you take a sip of water? What can I do?" she asked, trying so hard to make everything OK. "I don't know..." It was the truth. I wasn't OK, but nothing could make this better. Even my unborn baby, Adeline, was feeling the stress, offering strong kicks in protest against her dad's urn currently resting on my stomach. It was a terrible, tragic, and sad reality ... and it was ours.

Nate appeared, "Ashley, they're ready for you..." I heard him say gently.

I got up, bit my lower lip, clutched his arm for dear life and slowly started walking down the aisle. Officers in white uniforms on either side of the walkway saluted their brother in arms as we made our way toward the front of the chapel. I held on to Brian's urn as I sat down in the wooden pew. Isabel and Hudson sat next to me, and Adeline kicked me to remind me that she, too, was in this with us. I held his urn as our family and friends shared their own stories of love and laughter, moments shared with Brian that they'd cherish forever. I held it as the hot, wet tears slipped from my eyes and cascaded down my cheeks and settled in a puddle on its smooth surface. I held it as I was escorted outside to witness the three-volley salute, and I held it while our dear friend, who Brian and I affectionately referred to as Uncle Mike, read from a sheet of paper I'd handed him hours before and asked him to read aloud on my behalf. Uncle Mike, with his gregarious smile and Midwest-raised calm and kind demeanor, had answered Brian's Craigslist ad looking for a roommate to rent a room in our Gig Harbor house. Uncle Mike was living with Brian when I moved in, and had a front-row seat to our whirlwind relationship. He and his boyfriend, George, would quickly become some of our best friends, often staying up late with us on weekends sharing funny stories out by the firepit and discussing family drama or upcoming travels. Uncle Mike lived with us while we brought home Izzy and then Hudson, and though it was time, it was a sad day when he finally moved out. He had become a part of our family, a godfather to Hudson, the 'Will to my Grace' while Brian had been deployed and it was just he and I in the house, eating boxed macaroni and cheese and dancing around the living room to 80's music Brian would have been repulsed by. He was an important part of mine and Brain's lives, and he was the only person I wanted to read this for me; my final love letter to Brian.

June 2, 2018

My final love note to you, Brian.

In looking around our home these past two weeks I found the box in your bedside table of every love note I've ever written to you. Scribbled on scratch pieces of paper, notes from the many lunches I made you over the years, silly jokes I left around the house, cards I packed with you on deployments or trips away. There were hundreds and hundreds and hundreds of love notes in this box of yours, all from me and all with the intent of letting you know how much you mean to me every single chance I have. While I will never stop loving you, this will be my final love note written to you.

More than anything else I could ever say to you either in life or in death, I just want you to know how much I have loved you and how thankful I am for the life we built together. From the first time we met at 20 years old in the basement of your Division Street house in Portland, Oregon, to the morning of May 20th, 2018 when we stood in the doorway of the home we built together—even with (a lot) of time spent apart during some of those years, I've loved you every single moment during that time. I know you teased me about breaking up with you after six weeks of dating in 2003, but while I knew you were the right person for me, I wasn't ready to be married that young. Reconnecting with you 10 years later and being able to tell you I'd thought about you throughout those years and hearing you had thought about me—I knew without question after that first phone call that we would be married and live happily ever after together. It took exactly two weeks for us to realize the love we had previously had for one another was still there and we sat on the Oregon coast together, huddled under blankets at sunset as you told me you loved me. We would be married in this exact spot ten months later. We would later bring our two children to this exact spot and you have to trust me that I will bring Adeline to this spot as well as soon as I possibly can.

If there is anything I want to say to you, babe, it's thank you. I'm thankful to you for the memories, treasures, adventures, and, without question, incredible life you made possible for me. We were a team and partnership in every sense of the word. Each of us strong and capable on our own, but together we were unstoppable. In our wedding vows we promised to be each other's partners-in-crime in both life and death, and I won't forget that. Our children will know the incredible human being you were, how much you contributed to this world, to me, and to each of them. They will know the adventurous spirit you instilled in all those around you, not afraid or unwilling to try anything—encouraging others to set their fears aside so they could truly experience life. I'm thankful to you for this and that your children will grow up having this same type of attitude toward life and the world around us.

I also need you to know I'm sad. Devastated. Heartbroken. You and I both know and talked about often how we are the only people in the entire world for one another and that anything or anybody else would be just settling. Impossible to do when you've experienced perfection and love on this level. Thank you for showing me what love looks and feels like. For making me feel every single day that I'm the most special person in the world. I need you to know I'm not mad at you for leaving. I love you enough to be thankful that this is how your story ends, you went out doing exactly what you love and I have no question that you were thinking about me and our beautiful family. Please don't be upset or worry about me. I will cry and mourn for the life I wanted us to continue to have together, but not because I'm upset with you or what happened. As a true Captain would do, you went down with your ship and I love you even more for that as that's exactly who you are and who my heart belongs to. I know you'll always be coming back home to me.

I and Love and You.

Yours,

Ash

Chapter Three

Three weeks. That's all the time I had left to pack up my life and move off the island after Brian's funeral. I had gone back and forth on this decision, and I didn't want to stay. I couldn't stay. The thought of bringing our new baby home to a place that had only recently been a place of such joy in our lives now brought nothing but immense sadness and was unbearable to stay in any longer. Images of midnight feedings on the red couch in our living room, of Adeline napping in the corner of the bedroom I had weeks earlier shared with the dad she'd never get to meet, it was too much to imagine without him there with me. This home, our home, was full of memories of our life together and I couldn't handle it. I had to go.

"You and the kids can come stay with me, honey. Wait things out until you have Adeline and see how you're feeling after," Linda graciously offered. She knew I was struggling with what to do, where to go, and how exactly to get myself, my kids, and my dog all there before going into labor, but I had no solid plan. It wasn't just the dark brown house we'd called home for the past year that was hard to be in; it was the entire island of Oahu. Every twist and turn of the streets surrounding joint base Pearl Harbor–Hickam had memories tied to them, a fleeting image, a moment of time we'd shared as a family, and a vision cemented in my thoughts of happier days. Every palm tree served as a reminder of paradise and the incredible life Brian and I had shared together. "I can't believe we get to live here!" we'd exclaim time and time again to each other, our feet buried in the warm sun-bleached sand of the beach near our home. We'd watch the planes taking off from the nearby airport, carrying tourists away, people heading back to their homes, their lives and their routines. Not us though. Hawaii was ours and we felt just as much a part of it as it was now a part of us.

Hawaii would certainly be a part of our story forever, but now the time had come for us to leave it. I went on with my days in a haze, not cognizant of the minutes and hours passing by. I heard the conversations happening in my home, keenly aware they were about me and the kids, but unable to focus my attention to listen in or even respond to the questions being asked of me. My decision to leave the island brought with it a new question I didn't know how to answer: *Where will you go?*

Staying on the island wasn't an option, but I didn't have any answers past that. My mom wanted me to go with her to San Diego, my brothers offered up their homes in Texas and New Jersey, my childhood friends back home in Oregon and Washington sent out similar invitations, but I couldn't stomach the thought of any of it. Home was wherever Brian and I were together with our kids, and now I was going to have to figure out how to do this without him.

"Ash, come stay with us," Brian's sister, Nikki, offered. She had flown out immediately following his death and hadn't left my side in the weeks since. "We can move things around a little bit and make room. You can stay with us as long as you need to, OK? Please?" The offer was kind and incredibly generous. This wasn't a situation any of us had ever dreamed of being in, and Nikki and her husband, Aaron, already had two children and two dogs occupying their four-bedroom home in Boise, Idaho. Moving myself, my dog, and two—soon to be three—kids into their home would be chaos. "I just can't, Nik. You guys have your own lives going on, the kids, the dogs, the baby...I just...we just...we can't."

But Nikki wouldn't budge, reminding me that Terry and Frank lived close by, and we'd have support from the entire family in Boise. Terry and Frank had offered their own home to us, and I knew we needed to be close to them as much as they needed to be close to us as we figured out how to work through Brian's loss together. *But Idaho? I don't want to live in Idaho.* Even in extreme duress, I knew myself well enough to know I'd have a hard time in a landlocked state. The ocean had been a part of our family story for so long, I couldn't help but feel that moving there would be a betrayal to Brian and the way we had planned on raising our children together. During the course of our relationship, Brian and I had talked many times about how and where we wanted to raise our children, and Idaho had never come up as an option, unless it was preceded by the word "not." But I needed help. I was at the lowest point of my life, in unfathomable pain, and I knew I couldn't take care of myself, let alone my young children—while preparing to give birth to another. Despite our vast lifestyle differences, I trusted Nikki and knew she would take care of me, of us, and felt it was imperative for Izzy and Hudson to be surrounded by Brian's family members so they could hear stories about him, feel the love everyone had for him, see him in their mannerisms, and in his absence, get to know him through his family. "OK, Nik. If you'll have us, we'll come to Idaho," I finally whispered under my breath, feeling defeated, but grateful all at the same time.

Once the decision of *where* had been made, it was time to plan the move back to the mainland. What do I pack? *Aghhh! I have to pack. Where do I start? What do I need for the next few months? What can go in storage? What do the kids need? What will the baby need? What will fit in Nikki's house? I can't bring it all.* At some point my dad, Mike, who I'd had a strained relationship with over the previous ten years, but who I also knew I could call in a true time of need, who was afraid of flying, yet dropped everything to get to Hawaii to be with Hudson, Izzy and I, and who had also stayed on the island to help, went to Home Depot and purchased ten large black plastic storage containers with bright yellow lids to encourage me to begin the sorting process. Anything I could fit into these totes would be coming on the airplane with me as we left the island and everything else would be left behind to be packed by the military movers and put into storage until I had a place for them to send it. Pictures of Brian and our family, his navy uniforms, his favorite coffee mugs, love notes we had written to each other over the years—

anything that reminded me of him—made it into those totes. Clothes, shoes, toys, and books could all be replaced, but these items that he'd touched were irreplaceable and I didn't want them out of my sight.

No matter how much I willed the clock to stop moving, time was out of my control. I kept track of the passing days by watching beautiful bouquets of flowers from friends and family being delivered from around the world. A bouquet of birds of paradise delivered from Mo, Colette and Marina who I'd shared an apartment with in New York City in 2005, but who now lived in Australia, Portland and a van travelling the country, came to rest on my kitchen counter with a note expressing their condolences. White lilies from a wives club on base, yellow roses from a long-lost aunt in upstate New York, a beautiful houseplant from a family down the street who had walked past our house countless times while Brian and I were out front rinsing dive gear. The vases would sit on—then disappear from—the kitchen counter, with somebody in the house carefully watching the leaves change, discarding them before they, too, died. The days were excruciatingly long, but it all happened so fast and as soon as Brian's funeral was over, everyone's attention shifted to the health and welfare of baby Adeline, who still needed a few months to grow before joining us in person. I had a responsibility to our unborn baby to take care of her, but I was struggling. I couldn't eat. I couldn't sleep. I couldn't drink. The stress of this reality was taking a huge toll, and my body wasn't tolerating it well. I needed to go to the doctor, but I didn't want to. I just didn't care if she was OK, I didn't care if I was OK, I didn't want to do this anymore.

I don't care.

Last time I had been to my doctor's office was with Brian. We had driven the palm tree-lined winding roads of the Pali Highway together, making our way up the windward side of Oahu, holding hands as the warm breeze flowed freely through the open windows of our white pickup truck. We had done this same drive countless times together, always the same route, and always holding hands, talking excitedly about what we'd see at our appointment that day. "I can't believe we're having another daughter!" we'd cried excitedly together as our doctor confirmed Adeline would in fact be a little girl and would be joining our family in late August 2018. Brian held my hand during that appointment and every single one since, squeezing it tightly when the grainy image and flutter of her heartbeat flickered on the black-and-white ultrasound screen. Our *aloha* rainbow baby, the one we had so desperately wanted and had hoped for after suffering two devastating miscarriages. Brian had been there for it all, but now he wasn't. He wouldn't be coming to this appointment, or any after this. He wouldn't be holding my hand. He wouldn't be smiling back at me as I turned my head to see his reaction the moment baby Adeline appeared on the ultrasound screen, and he wouldn't be there when I saw her appear in my arms just a few months later.

No, I didn't want to go.

"Ashley, honey, we really need to get you to the doctor, just to make sure she's doing OK." Nikki and Terry said in unison.

Doing OK? I don't think you understand. I don't care if she's OK. I'm not OK. I can't do this. You don't get it...I'm really not OK. Brian won't be able to see her, he'll never get to hold her. She'll never even get to meet him. Her own dad. How is this real? It's too much. I don't want to do this. I don't want to have her. This isn't fair.

But I had to.

I forced myself to go to the doctor, with Nikki and Terry by my side. As soon as the doctor stepped into the room, she took one look at me and began sobbing.

"I'm so sorry..." she was able to say, as she wrapped her arms around me. "I just can't believe it...I remember your first appointment with me and the way you looked at each other when you first heard her heartbeat, I know how excited he was for this baby, the way he held your hand..." she couldn't finish her sentence.

I was numb. My heart was broken, and I was full of sadness, heartache, loss, and grief, but also pregnant with a baby living and growing inside of me. Every emotion seemed to be in competition with the other, and it was up to me to sort through it all. I was losing control—I had lost control—and I felt empty. This would be my final child, the last time my body would carry a baby, a baby we had wanted so badly, the baby who would complete our family, and yet there I was in the doctor's office, and I just wanted it to end. I felt the familiar sting of tears in my eyes, the wet sensation pooling up behind my eyelids searching for an escape, just as I was. I didn't know what to say. I blinked to release the tears and hugged her back.

I slowly glanced at Nikki and Terry, standing to my left, who had tears in their own eyes as they quietly watched this exchange take place.

"Would you like to see her?" the doctor asked after wiping her eyes and typing something into the sonogram machine.

No, I don't. Seeing her will somehow acknowledge this is real, that she's real, that this is happening. I don't want this to be real.

"Okay," I heard myself whisper. This was the first time that Nikki and Terry would be seeing Addy and I wanted them to have this, a moment of time connected to Brian, even if it was through my belly and appeared in the form of an ultrasound photo. I knew they needed this and that Brian would have wanted to share it with them.

I slowly leaned back and allowed my head to rest on the cold exam table pillow, as I uncovered my protruding belly and let the doctor spread the warm gel on me. I closed my eyes and turned my head away. I didn't want to see the baby. As soon as I heard Terry gasp and sigh, I knew they could see her. I turned my head even further away as the tears flooded my eyes, pooling on the thin paper protector covering the table below me. I couldn't—I didn't—want to see her without Brian. I wasn't going to make it another two months like this. *I can't do it. I don't want to do it. I won't survive this.*

Christmas Morning; 2017

"I have one more Christmas present for you, babe." I told Brian as he came upstairs to check on me in bed. I'd had to excuse myself from the festivities downstairs because I wasn't feeling well, but I had an idea as to why and wanted to go upstairs to see if it was real. I took the last pregnancy test I had remaining in my drawer and watched in delight as the second pink line appeared. Positive. We'd suffered two devastating miscarriages in

the previous months, but I felt deep inside this one was different. I knew it was going to stick.

"You're kidding..." he said, cautiously, but with a smile forming on his face. He was nervous because of the torment we'd just gone through with the loss of our previous pregnancies, but it was hard to not be excited at this sight.

"Merry Christmas, babe," I smiled. We'd find out eight weeks later we'd be having a girl, and shortly after that, we'd settle on the name Adeline Makai. Makai meant 'toward the sea' in Hawaiian and was a name special to the two of us.

"Ashley, you need to eat," my doctor cut through my thoughts as she finished her exam. "Even if you don't feel like eating or drinking, try sipping a milkshake or a smoothie throughout the day. Honey, you need to keep something in you." She was gentle but firm, both a medical professional and a human being who recognized the extent of my grief and the delicate position I was in.

I was losing weight when I should have been gaining it. My blood pressure was elevated. My doctor was concerned, rightfully so, but I didn't care.

"Honey, you have gestational hypertension, which could lead to pre-eclampsia." She finally said.

She talked through the risks of pre-eclampsia with Terry and Nikki while I sat there, listening as the words went in one ear and out the other. "Seizures, kidney failure, potential danger, or even death for mom and baby if not monitored." She went on, watching me for any sign that I was listening to what she was saying. *I wasn't.* I had checked out, welcoming the thought of any and all of those things happening to me as a means to an end, anything to take this pain away.

"I'm worried about you," my doctor said as she wiped the gel off my stomach. "I want to make sure you have the support you need in Idaho."

Nikki had spent the week prior calling obstetricians in Boise on my behalf, explaining my situation and trying to find somebody who would take me on as a patient. "She'll be thirty-one weeks pregnant. Moving to Boise from Hawaii. High-risk pregnancy. Recent emotional trauma. Military insurance..."

"No, she needs to see her regular doctor," they'd say.

"Well, you see, we are in an unfortunate situation because her husband, my brother..." and Nikki was forced to tell the same story over and over again to every receptionist who wouldn't agree to schedule me an appointment. It must have been torturous for her. She was grieving the death of her brother, yet she was supporting me, making sure I was safe, showing unconditional love, taking care of so many things I wasn't even aware of, and trying her best to take care of Izzy and Hudson while I couldn't.

Time was still ticking by. The black totes were now packed and sealed. The once beautiful flower bouquets lining my countertop were now dried up and sitting outside waiting to be discarded. My dad had flown home with my dog, Chance; the cattle dog-lab mix Brian and I had adopted from a rescue on Valentine's Day weekend 2013. We had only been dating a few weeks, but intrinsically knew we were going to be together, and made the potentially wreckless-turned-best decision to adopt a dog together. Chance had been my constant companion throughout each of Brian's deployments, through pregnancies, and through bringing Izzy and Hudson home. With a storied past of his own, he'd survived a move across ocean with us, a false-nuclear missile scare, tugs on his ears and tail from the kids, changing climates, houses and lifestyles, yet, here he was, my tried and true, getting ready to leave the island with a one-way ticket booked from Honolulu to Boise. For Chance and me, things were changing again and it was time to say goodbye.

I took one final walk through the hallways of our home at 3073 Bridges Street, closing my eyes and remembering the laughter that had filled them weeks prior. I walked down the stairs and pictured Brian standing there, arms outstretched as he had done on Christmas morning. I walked past the red couch in our living room and cried as I thought about the memories we'd made as a family in these exact spots, and then I walked toward the front door. Our little wooden sign with *E Komo Mai* hung from a single nail in the center of it, offering a Hawaiian "welcome" to all who entered our home, now saying goodbye as I walked away. Nate was waiting for me on the porch with a few final pieces of paperwork to sign so he could handle the rest of the move on my behalf, but more importantly, he offered a heartfelt goodbye hug as I cried, sincerely thanking him for everything he had done for the kids and I the past month. And just like that, it was time to go. Linda, Robert, Brian's boss, Jason, and wife, Carolyn, piled me and the kids into their truck for the half-mile trip to the airport, while a handful of friends, the kids' Hawaiian nanny, Victoria, a young military spouse herself, whom we lovingly referred to as V", and Brian's coworkers followed behind us to say *a hui hou*—"until we meet again."

I approached the Alaska Airlines counter with tears in my eyes. I clutched the green bag containing Brian's urn in my arms as tightly as I could. I hadn't let him out of my sight since I'd collected it from the funeral home, and I didn't plan to anytime soon. He'd be flying with me to Boise. The airline representative glanced from my bloodshot eyes and swollen face to the green bag, a puzzled expression on her face, obviously aware that whatever was in that bag was upsetting me. "Where are you flying today ma'am?" I looked up at her and started to say "Boise ..." but couldn't keep it together a moment longer. The reality of my situation hit me like a tidal wave. *Boise. I don't want to go to Boise. I don't want to leave our home. I don't want to do this. I want Brian.* Tears were coming in so fast that they fogged my vision, and I was suddenly lightheaded. Linda walked closer to me, placed her arms around me, and helped me step away from the counter to catch my breath. Eric, Brian's coworker, walked up to the counter to take over the conversation and explain what was going on.

"I'm so sorry..." she said, looking from the green bag to my pregnant belly, to Izzy and Hudson, and back to me. She was so kind in that moment, offering to wave the luggage fee of every single black tote we'd dragged in, filled to the brim with my most sentimental possessions. "Best wishes to you and your family, ma'am," she said as she handed me back my military ID, recently reissued with "sponsor status: deceased" in the upper right corner.

We walked as a group toward the security line, and I braced myself for these goodbyes. Linda, Robert, V, and Carolyn were some of the people who had held my hand tightly the past month, who had been a part of mine and Brian's lives in Hawaii, and who hadn't left my side, but whose sides I now had to leave. "Is Dadda going to meet us in Boise?" Izzy asked as we started hugging everyone goodbye, turning an already excruciating experience into a moment frozen in time. "No honey, he's not, but we will come back to Hawaii every single year to remember him, OK?" I offered as I stifled my tears, my friends doing their best to hold back their own. Izzy, Hudson, and V gave each other one final hug goodbye. Linda wrapped her arms around me and told me to be strong, that I "got this." With that, we walked away. Holding on to the green bag with one hand, my pregnant belly with the other, and with Hudson, Izzy, and Nikki by my side, we said goodbye to paradise, to the people who made it so, and to life as I had known it. The remains of Brian were in my arms, but our last memories of him would be left on this island, and it was excruciating to leave.

I don't want to do this, please just let me die here with Brian.

Chapter Four

"We're making our initial descent into the Seattle area and should have you on the ground in about twenty minutes," the captain announced cheerfully from the cockpit as we felt the plane beginning to turn. I was exhausted past recognition, but I had heard this announcement crystal clear and my eyes shot up desperately searching to make eye contact with Nikki who was sitting across the aisle from me. *Seattle? No! We have a layover at the Sea-Tac airport?* I had been so oblivious to the happenings around me in the weeks leading up to this moment, I had somehow missed the fact we'd have to stop here on our way to Idaho.

The Seattle-Tacoma international airport had become a home away from home over the past five years for me and Brian, and I wasn't ready to see it. We had spent countless hours at this airport together, sitting side by side in the wooden rocking chairs in front of the giant picture windows overlooking the tarmac, planning for our future together as we counted down the minutes to his next six-month submarine deployment. This had been our home airport, the gray-speckled flooring soon becoming as familiar as those in our own house. We'd spent hours walking the tile-lined hallways waiting for airplanes that took our family on trips around the world. I had kissed Brian goodbye at this gate, I had welcomed him home at this security checkpoint, we got a little tipsy together at that restaurant while waiting to board our plane bound for a new adventure. Between the two of us, we flew in and out of Sea-Tac nearly once a month and had created memories in just about every corner of it, and I wasn't ready to see it, to confront such a visual representation of home without him here.

"I'm so sorry, Ash. We have an hour layover here before our flight to Boise," Nikki offered gently, sensing I was having a hard time with the unexpected stop as she reached over to hold my hand from across the aisle. The tears poured down my cheeks as the plane touched down, the yellow runway lights illuminating the shadows of the towering evergreen trees surrounding the airport. Hudson stirred next to me, jarred awake from the sudden *whoosh* of the wheels hitting the ground. "Mama?" He looked up in a moment of slight panic, meeting my gaze, then reassured I was still with him, fell back to sleep. The *whoosh* meant we were here, and a few minutes later we pulled into our gate. I held my sweet boy, still groggy with sleep, in one arm, as I reached out for Izzy with my other, Brian in the green bag slung over my shoulder and held tightly in place as Hudson rested his head above it. I took a deep breath, tears still cascading down my cheeks, and put one foot in front of the other as we stepped off the airplane that had just taken us away from our Hawaiian home.

The sixty minutes spent in that airport were excruciatingly painful and long. Everywhere I turned, I saw Brian. My eyes were bloodshot and my vision cloudy, but the images of our life together were crystal clear. *We flew to Portugal as a family out of this gate. We flew home from San Diego at this one. We moved to Hawaii out of that one over there.* And now here was another memory created at the Sea-Tac international airport, only this one I wish I didn't have.

I walked slowly, holding my two children, the tangible representation of the love Brian and I had for each other, carrying the green bag with my beloved husband's ashes, with his sister by my side. My head hung low, my eyes failed to focus on the steps I was taking, and my sight was partially blocked by my protruding belly.

"Do you want to take a break? Sit down for a minute?" Nikki asked, looking at me to make sure I was still with her, both physically and emotionally. She knew this was excruciating and she'd made it her sole responsibility to get me to Boise, safely.

"I'm not okay, Nik." I said.

"I know, Ash. I'm so sorry." Nikki responded. There was nothing else she could say or do.

I spent the next hour of my life reliving the many memories created in this airport, watching my children doing their best to stay patient and calm, watching the clock wind down, until soon enough, "All passengers headed to Boise, please board now," was announced and we once again boarded another plane, taking us away from home. The eighty-minute flight from Seattle to Boise took forever. I was exhausted. The kids were exhausted. Nikki was exhausted. None of us wanted to be doing any of this, but here we were, stepping off yet another airplane, at nearly midnight. We walked together as a family out the double doors, down the escalator and toward baggage claim where somebody had already stacked ten black plastic totes with bright yellow lids against the wall, ASHLEY BUGGE, BOISE, IDAHO printed in big black letters across the side. *This can't be happening. I don't want to be here. I don't want to do this. How is this real? I just want to die. When will this nightmare be over?*

I wept the entire ride to Nikki and her husband Aaron's house, while Izzy and Hudson slept soundly, seated next to me in the family minivan. Aaron had rearranged the furniture in their four-bedroom home to accommodate us. He bought and assembling new beds for the kids, moved their own kids into a single bedroom, and cleaned out the office to make room for me, and soon-to-be-born Adeline, and Chance, who would be joining us shortly. They had gone above and beyond, no questions asked, no expense spared, and opened their arms and home to us. I was beyond thankful to them for taking us in, and thankful that Brian's parents would also be right down the street...yet, moving to Boise felt like salt in an open wound. I didn't want to be here. Every streetlight we passed, every twist and turn of the roads leading through rural America reminded me that we weren't in Hawaii anymore. *This* was our new reality.

We pulled in the driveway of their suburban home. An American flag was proudly displayed in the front yard, all ready for the upcoming Fourth of July holiday. Frank helped unload the black totes from his truck and stacked them in a single corner of the already full garage. "Where do I start?" I looked around, asking nobody in particular. It was late, and we were all past the point of exhaustion. "Do you know which one the pajamas are in, Nik?" I looked at her, weary and not sure if I had even packed any, for myself or the kids.

"Your doctor appointment is early tomorrow morning," Nikki gently reminded me as she put her arm around me, a fresh set of tears in my eyes at the sight of our belongings crammed into these plastic totes now on the floor of her garage. "Try to get some rest, and I'll get the kids to bed."

She had managed to find an obstetrician willing to see me, and booked my first appointment for the following morning, nine hours after we became residents of Boise, Idaho. I didn't want to go. *They're going to want to see her...*I thought. *They're going to ask why I moved at thirty-one weeks pregnant, where my husband is, what brought me here from Hawaii...I don't want to talk about it. I can't do this by myself.* Brian was gone. I wanted to be gone too. This pain was too real. *I don't want to face this. I don't want to have this baby. Not anymore. I'm ready to be done.* I said goodnight and made my way to the office-turned-guest room at the end of the hallway, too tired and too distraught to even change out of the clothes I'd just traveled across the ocean in. I was exhausted in every sense of the term, my body in a haze and my brain unable to compute the reality happening around me. I laid in bed with the lights off, listening to the shuffling of feet on the hardwood floors outside my door, the hushed whispers of adults and tired children as they tried to get settled into their rooms for the night. I just needed to get through this night, I needed sleep, I needed to wake with a clear mind, and to re-evaluate our situation. My heart was broken, but my body and brain still worked, and I knew I just needed to get some rest. I closed my eyes, but the light from the hallway peeked in under the wood framed guest room door and cast shadows throughout the room. I used that light to look around my new room, where I could see a desk in the corner, a bookshelf to my left, a baby travel crib near the closet, ready for baby Adeline whenever she got here, and finally a nightstand to my right—which I'd perched Brian's urn on when I'd first walked into the room. Now laying on my right side, I shifted my body to face his urn, immediately feeling the warmth of my tears collecting on the speckled white-green pillowcase my head was resting on. *Babe. I miss you. I can't do this without you.* I spoke to the little brass box holding the remains of my husband. *You don't understand, Brian. I really can't do this without you. You promised me I could die first...you knew I couldn't live without you. You don't understand how sad I am.* I'd been in the fight of my life for a month already, and it wasn't getting any easier. We'd made it to Boise, my kids were safe, nearly asleep down the hall of their Aunt Nikki and Uncle Aaron's house, and this had been the goal. For the first time in over a month, I was alone with my thoughts. I laid in the bed of that guest room and let the darkness seep in.

I want out of this pain.

I can't do this.

I don't want to do this.

This is too much for one person.

I don't want to die...I just don't want to live.

Please just let me have a heart attack right now.

I can't take care of the two kids I have, let alone a newborn.

What if...what if I take myself out of this before the baby is born, Nikki would only have to take care of Izzy and Hudson and she could do it...

I just want the pain to stop.

There were sleeping pills in my backpack. One of the few things I'd made sure to pack before leaving Hawaii.

It would be pain-free. I could just fall asleep and never wake up again.

While still lying in bed, I reached my hand out to Brian's urn, feeling its cold and smooth surface against my fingertips, visualizing the contents within. I closed my eyes and pictured him on the metal hospital bed when I last saw him. He still had the IV in his arm and the breathing tube in his mouth. I pictured somebody in a white lab coat wheeling him down to the autopsy room, wondering if they had taken the time to admire the colorful tattoos on his arms and legs before cutting into him. I pictured them going down the list of organs I'd consented to the donation of, taking them from his cold body—just another day at work for them. I pictured them wheeling what was left of him to the incinerator, the stack of love letters I'd written him over the years and had delivered to the mortuary to be cremated with him, placed on his chest as somebody lit the fire. I pictured him being cremated, the last look on his face, the dimple on his left cheek slowly fading away, the love letters now a plume of smoke as his body gave way to the heat. And now the remains of all of that, the remains of my love, of Brian, tightly secured in a plastic bag inside of this brass urn on my nightstand. I was sick to my stomach. I reached for the bottle of sleeping pills and held it in my hand.

How many would it take to make sure I didn't wake up? I wouldn't have to live in this sadness anymore. I wouldn't have to face life without Brian. This baby would never have to face life without her dad. She'd never have to experience life with a heartbroken mother incapable of taking care of her. This is too much for one person to have to deal with. I'm ready. I just want this to be over.

I stared at the bottle, visualizing the small blue pills inside, knowing if ingested in extreme quantity, would finally put a stop to my sadness. They stared back at me, enticing me to grab them all at once, throw them in my mouth, and swallow them. They promised me relief. I reached for the bottle, shaking it slightly just to guess how many there were.

That would probably be enough.

What if it's not and someone finds me and tries to revive me? Should I leave a note so they know? To please just let me go?

Do I say goodbye to Izzy and Hudson? What if Addy somehow lives through this? Do I write her a note too? What do I say besides, "I'm sorry."

My thoughts drifted. I pictured Izzy and Hudson sleeping in the room next to mine. Izzy with her pink blanket and Hudson with his stuffed bear protecting them. They'd been through so much this past month.

This would be their story forever. My dad drowned, and a month later my mom killed herself. Can I do that to them? This will set me free. I just want it to be over.

I glanced at the bottle, willing myself to place them back in my backpack.

Not tonight. I can't do that to them tonight. Maybe tomorrow?

I needed to see Izzy and Hudson. I ran my fingers again across Brian's urn before getting out of bed. One foot in front of the other, I walked down the hall, the glow from the nightlight in the bathroom illuminating the hallway on my way to the kids' room. I opened the door and peered inside to see my two beautiful children sound asleep.

What a day. What a life. These poor kids.

I reached down and rubbed my belly. *Adeline. My sweet Addy girl..*

Can I do this? Can we do this? It's going to be you and me baby girl, we're in this together.

I felt nauseous. We had wanted this baby so bad. All of them. This was our family, our dream. But it had taken Brian and I both to make it all happen and now he was gone.

I can't do it all by myself. They're so young. Izzy's only three, Hudson just turned two, and Addy isn't even born yet.

I walked back down the hall to my room and got in bed. *Not tonight.* That much was decided, so instead, I wept. I don't know how it was possible to have any tears left inside of me, but I let it all out, my pillow catching every ounce of heartache and sadness that spouted from my eyes. *I'm pregnant. I'm a widow. I want to die. I'm feeling sorry for myself. I'm...*

"Ash?" Nikki interrupted my thoughts as she appeared in my doorway.

"Yeah" I asked, clearing my voice.

"Are you OK? Can I come in?" Nikki had spent the past month by my side, and it was silly of me to assume our first night in her home would have been any different.

"I'm not OK, Nik." I leaned in as she sat next to me on my bed, wrapping her arms around me.

"I know, Ash. I'm so sorry. I wish I could take this pain away for you. You're the strongest person I know, and I know you can do this. Izzy and Hudson and Addy need you to do this. They need their mom," she added, sensing this moment was different.

I can't do it, Nik.

Nikki, with her tall frame and striking resemblance to her brother—my husband—sat with me for the next thirty minutes, holding me in her arms like one of her own children as I wept, eventually becoming drowsy enough to fall asleep. "I'll see you in a couple of hours," she said gently, tilting her head toward my belly, "we should leave here by 8:30 to get to your appointment on time. I'm here with you, Ash, I'm not going anywhere."

***

"Mrs. Bugge," the nurse said, "your blood pressure is a little high."

I nodded. What else could I say? This was my third visit to the doctor this week and the third time a nurse told me this. I'd had a sleepless and restless night—yet again. Izzy and Hudson caught a bug at some point during our first few days in Boise and weren't feeling well. They slept in my bed the night before, and while I was supposed to be taking it easy during these final weeks of my pregnancy, two sick kids required a lot of care and attention. I'd been advised to stay on bed rest in an attempt to bring down my blood pressure, but the reality of my situation was that I just couldn't.

"I know you've got a lot on your plate at home, but we really need to get you to thirty-five weeks to prevent Adeline ending up in the NICU. Are you taking it easy?" my doctor asked as he looked at my latest vitals. I nodded "yes" while Nikki shook her head "no." It didn't matter anyway, the past few weeks we'd been in Boise, I had come to peace with the idea that I wouldn't actively try to take my own life, but I wouldn't be upset if something happened to me in the process.

"We'd like to run some tests and keep you under observation." The doctor suggested. He'd taken a special liking to Nikki and me, having delivered our sister-in-law's babies and also having been briefed on the circumstances that brought me to Idaho. "I'd like to see you every three days to check on you and the baby. Given your situation, it's best to keep a close eye on you because I think we'll be looking at the potential of preterm labor."

Nikki and I drove back to her house in silence, now fully aware of the fact my body was no longer tolerating this pregnancy well and at any one of these future appointments, the doctor could tell me I'd have to stay in the hospital until Adeline was born. We got home and I called Kayla, the nanny I had recently hired for Izzy and Hudson who was scheduled to start with us on Monday.

"In search of a nanny to help with my two—and soon to be three—children," my advertisement began. "Moving to Boise from Hawaii and need somebody to start as soon as possible." The photo in the corner of my profile displayed a family of four—Brian, me, Izzy, and Hudson—all smiling happily toward the camera, an image captured on one of our final days spent in Gig Harbor, Washington, together before we moved to Hawaii. We used this profile to hire our nanny in Hawaii, and I'd considered changing the photo before putting up the new ad for Boise, but I wasn't ready to face the reality that our new family photo wouldn't include Brian.

I quickly received a reply from a young woman named Kayla. Born and raised in Idaho, she had no previous nannying experience, but she often babysat for her niece and said she would love the opportunity to nanny for my family. I really liked Kayla as a potential nanny, and I didn't want to scare her away by revealing too much about our personal situation during that first phone interview, so I scheduled an in-person interview a few days after landing in Boise, deciding I could fill her in then.

"Hi, I'm Kayla!" she said, reaching out to shake my hand. She had thick, full eyelashes and a sweet demeanor, and I had a feeling she was going to run for the hills once I explained everything to her.

"My husband passed away. Diving accident. Seven months pregnant. Military family. Izzy—age three. Hudson—age two. Living here now. Sister-in-law's house. Eight people, three dogs. Not all mine. Full-time help. Hospital stays. Chaos. Potential for travel..." I was crying. She was crying. We sat outside in the Boise summer heat and cried together as I told her who we were and what I needed. I finally got through it and when I was done, I was afraid she was going to shake my hand and close the door behind her to a future that didn't involve dealing with me and my desperate situation. Instead, she smiled and said, in the sweetest tone possible, "I'm so sorry you had to go through all of that. I'd love to work for you and your family."

"OK," I said, almost in a questioning tone. "When can you start?" I knew in that moment she'd forever become a part of our family story.

"Can I give two weeks to my current job?" she asked.

"Of course." I smiled through my tears. "Um, the only thing is, there's potential I go see the doctor one of these days and they don't let me come home. If that happens, I might have to call you in the middle of the night to come watch Izzy and Hudson while I'm giving birth to Adeline."

There, now she's going to run away for sure.

"No problem," she said, again with that warm smile. I thanked her and we set her start date for two weeks later.

"Alright kiddo, we need to chat for a minute. Today's tests show you've got a little protein in your urine and your blood pressure isn't coming down as we'd hoped to see." The doctor was trying to be gentle with me, while also conveying the gravity of my situation. "Last week we ordered your labs for gestational diabetes and it looks like they came back with elevated numbers, so we need to come up with a plan here."

Uh-huh.

"Today's numbers, coupled with all of your other symptoms, tell me you've got pre-eclampsia, which we've talked about and you understand can be very dangerous for you and your baby. Your kidneys are showing signs of distress, and your situation has the potential to go downhill very quickly. I want to prepare you for the idea that we're going to have to deliver her soon." He placed his hand on my shoulder as a way to highlight his care, but also his concern. "We're going to keep a very close eye on you, and I'm not going to let anything happen to you, OK? I'm not going to compromise your health, but you've already been through so much and we want to keep your baby out of the NICU if possible, so we're going to try hard to get you to the thirty-five-week mark before we induce you. We're going to try a couple of things and hope to hold her off for a few more days, OK?"

I went home and tried to focus on everything the doctor told me. It was happening. Whether I was ready for it or not, I was going to have to face labor and delivery soon, and this time Brian wouldn't be there for it. Nighttime came and the kids were sound asleep in my bed—not wanting me out of their eyesight, day or night, as they processed their own grief in losing their dad. I, on the other hand, couldn't fall asleep. So, I began writing again.

It's 1:08 a.m. here in Meridian, Idaho, and today was an emotional day. My mind is racing, my legs are restless, and even after 9 mg of melatonin and six consecutive episodes of Flipping Out, I still can't sleep. Today I went into the doctor for my routine appointment, and a nurse I haven't met before checked me in. She was making small talk and asked where I came from and why I moved here from Hawaii. I told her I moved here to be close to family and hoped to end the conversation at that. She then told me her friend moved here from Hawaii because her husband had retired from the military and asked if my husband was military also. I froze. It felt like it had just four weeks ago when I checked in for the first time and was asked my marital status and I couldn't bring myself to say the word "widow," so I just stood at the counter and cried and made the front desk girl feel incredibly uncomfortable until Nikki explained my situation. I don't know what triggers the tears these days, but it doesn't take much, and once I've had my first cry of the day it's all downhill from there. The doctor gave me a steroid shot to strengthen Adeline's lungs in preparation for a premature delivery next week and I have to have a second shot tomorrow. He also put me on a small dose of blood pressure medication to hopefully hold off these symptoms; however, ninety minutes after taking it I was shaky and lightheaded. I felt as if I would pass out and my BP was down to 118/56. I'm scared to take another dose until I see the doc tomorrow and talk to him about it. At this point, I feel like there is no good answer. I want to keep Adeline safe and growing and I certainly don't want to be spending any time with her in the NICU, but I'm losing confidence daily that I'm capable of doing that. My body is telling me I need to get this baby out of here, but I'm not emotionally ready for her. This is the last thing I have that is keeping these entire nine weeks somewhat of a distraction. As long as she's in there, I don't feel like I have to completely deal with losing Brian because the rest of our lives without him haven't started yet. Once she's here, that's it. I'm a single mom with three kids and together we have to navigate how to be a family without a husband and without a father and I don't want to do that.

I was thirty-four weeks and five days pregnant the night my doctor told me I wouldn't be going home until I gave birth. My blood pressure was well outside the range of safe for the baby and me, and she was exhibiting signs of distress.

"We're going to keep you here, kiddo." He said when I arrived for my fetal non-stress test.

Just like that, they strapped a band to my wrist, hooked me up to various monitors, and we started waiting for my body to fail me. It didn't take long. I'd been on hospital-monitored bedrest for fewer than twelve hours, when suddenly it began. Mid-conversation with Nikki, the room started to spin and I became lightheaded. I laid back in the hospital bed and closed my eyes to rest, but when I opened them, I couldn't see. "Something's wrong. I can't see, Nik. Nik, I can't see! Nik!" I panicked and reached out for Nikki, who had spent the night in the chair next to me and hadn't left my side since receiving the news I wouldn't be going home until Adeline was in my arms. Nikki pressed the call light, and the nurse came in immediately. "I think something is wrong." My voice cracked as I choked back tears and told the nurse my vision was blurry. My doctor had predicted this; my body was shutting down and it was happening very quickly. The nurse called my doctor who said, "Right now, start the induction," so with Nikki by my side and a photo of Brian in my hand, I was wheeled into the labor and delivery room.

"Honey, do you know if you'll want an epidural?" the nurse asked me.

"Yes," I said through tears. I was scared, and in such emotional distress, the thought of the physical pain accompanying childbirth was too much to consider.

"OK, sweetheart. I'll call our anesthesiologist and let her know. She's been working here for twenty-five years and she's the best. You're in good hands," she said while hanging a small bag labeled "Magnesium" from the IV rack next to my bed. "This is probably going to burn a little bit, but we need to get your blood pressure down before we start the Pitocin to kickstart your contractions. "It's ten o'clock now, I'll start this slow, and I think we can make it to thirty-five weeks," she said with a wink.

She was right. With every drip from the IV line, the magnesium felt like fire shooting through the veins in my hands. Not soon enough, the bag was emptied, and a new bag in its place, this time the contents labeled Pitocin. It wasn't long after she began the Pitocin drip that my contractions began, and I asked for the epidural. The anesthesiologist came in and introduced herself, asking if I had any questions. I'd had an epidural with both Izzy and Hudson, so I was familiar with what to expect. I said, "No, I think I'm OK," and I sat up, legs off the bed, Nikki in front of me to help me hold the position, anticipating a big pinch and then sweet relief from the pain.

There it was, the bee-sting sensation and then, "Where do you feel that?" the anesthesiologist asked me.

I was confused. The needle was in my back. In my spine to be more precise and I had writhed in pain at the sensation of it entering my body. Sensing my confusion, she repeated: "Where did you feel the pinch? Right side or left side?"

"Oh," I said trying to figure out where I felt it. "To the right, I think?"

"OK," she said cautiously. "I'm not sure I have it, I'm going to flush it."

I wasn't sure what that meant, but moments later I found out, and it hit me like a freight train. My head started spinning, my ears plugged and instantly felt like they were about to burst, my body went slack as I lost control and slumped into Nikki. I was going to pass out.

"Nikki!" I cried. "Nikki!"

"I missed it, I missed it," said the anesthesiologist.

"Something's wrong, I'm not OK..." I was crying now and slumped over in Nikki's arms with my heart thumping and emotions skyrocketing. I had not been prepared for my body to react like that, and I assumed the anesthesiologist made a grave error and that was it for me. I was going to die on the table right then. In a flash I began thinking of who was going to take care of my children, even my unborn one, if I did die. I couldn't leave them orphans. This was not how their lives were supposed to end up. This could not be their story: three children losing both father and mother in a matter of nine weeks. I had made it through that terrible first night in Boise, a bottle of sleeping pills in my hand, and if I had pulled through that, there was no way I was going to let myself die now. No. No!

"Ashley," Nikki said in the calmest tone she could manage, but I saw fear flash through her eyes as she looked to my nurse for reassurance. "I'm here, Ash. I'm here."

"Ashley, honey," the nurse came closer, looking me in the eyes. "You're not going to die sweetheart. That was a flush of adrenaline to see if she had the catheter in the right place. This is a normal reaction your body is having and you'll feel better in just a minute, but I need you to take some deep breaths with me."

"I'm so sorry," the anesthesiologist said, still standing behind me. The spinning in my head began subsiding and I managed to sit back up on my own. "I'm going to try again," she said after I'd managed to calm down a bit.

"Here we go, big pinch," she said as I felt the burn of the needle penetrate my back. I could feel the pressure of the foreign object in my spine as she moved it around trying to find the right placement, but she was silent during the procedure. And then, "Oh no...Nikki, no!" The same thing happened again. My ears filled with the pressure of a thousand rubber bands snapping, my head began spinning, and I lost control of my body yet again as I slumped forward into Nikki's arms. This time I knew that I wasn't going to die, but that didn't make the experience any less frightening or painful.

"I'm so sorry," she apologized again. "I'm going to try it one more time, a little to the left." She said, missing again, but this time realizing it before doing another adrenaline flush, and I got one more "I'm so sorry," before she said, "I'm going to call the other anesthesiologist so he can try."

"I am so sorry, sweetheart," said the nurse, holding my hand. "I've been here fifteen years and I've never seen a miss like that. Are you OK? Do you want to continue?"

"It's OK, I know everyone here knows my story and it's probably making people nervous. I don't think I can get through this without the epidural, can you call the other one but not tell him about me?" I asked her. This nurse had been with me on and off throughout my stay at the hospital and we had formed a special bond through the process. I trusted her and I knew she wasn't going to let anything bad happen to me in her care.

The other anesthesiologist came in, introduced himself, had me lean forward to expose my spine, and before I knew it had happened, I heard, "Thank you, you're all set!" and he was done. I looked up at Nikki who was smiling, relieved it was over. Once

I was finally able to lie back down, contractions picked up, and while I couldn't feel them, we tracked them through the monitor I had been hooked up to and watched them progress, knowing it was all about to happen.

"You're six centimeters dilated and doing great," my doctor let me know on a stop into my room later that morning. "You've also officially made it to thirty-five weeks, so no mandatory NICU time for Adeline as long as she's doing OK! Good job, mama." He smiled. He'd been in this with me the past month and was just as relieved as I was knowing we'd made it to this point.

An hour after he left, I felt a familiar sensation and knew it was about to happen.

"I think she's ready," I told my nurse who was in the room with me.

"Like, right now?" she asked, quickly turning to look at me to gauge just how ready I was.

"No, not this very second, but soon." I said, and before the words had finished leaving my lips, there was a sudden flash in the room as the overhead lights were turned on, the sound of a cart being wheeled toward me, a smaller, infant-sized one next to that, and out of the corner of my eye I watched as a team of two, three, four people in scrubs walked in the room, having been summoned in the event things didn't go as planned for Adeline or me. We were in this together, an unstoppable team who had already lived through the worst possible experience, and on the verge of meeting in person for the first time.

"Nikki, I need him, I don't want to do this without him." I said as I braced myself to begin pushing. I held Brian's photo to my chest, the same photo I'd used for his funeral cards and obituary, in his scuba diving suit, smiling, the dimple on his left check prominent as he beamed toward the camera. This photo made me happy and sad at the same time, and it was now all that I had of him to help me through the birth of his last child, a daughter. I held it tightly and started crying. Wailing. I didn't want this to be our story. I didn't want this to be our life. My life. The life of our babies. I sobbed. Nikki grabbed my hand, squeezing with all of her might as she fought back her own tears. My nurse walked over to blot my eyes with tissue, saving one for herself as the tears flowed down her cheeks as well.

"Alright, Ashley," said the doctor, now officially ready to help me welcome Adeline. "You're in charge here and you can do this. We're all here to help you, you tell me when you're ready and we're going to introduce you to your daughter. Are you ready? Deep breath and... push!"

One, two, three

I can't...I don't want to...Brian...I'm too sad...

Six, seven, eight

"Good, good! You're doing great, Ashley." the doctor said, his voice catching as he was holding back his own tears.

Ten.

I stopped pushing.

"Ashley, she's so close!" the doctor said, "give me half of a push and she's out!"

What!

I grabbed Nikki's hand tighter, this was all happening so fast and was suddenly so real. I took another deep breath and began pushing and counting again.

Three, four, five

"Reach down and grab your daughter, sweetheart," said the doctor.

"What?" I cried, hearing his voice but unable to see him through my tears.

"She's here, just help her out. Grab her under her arms and pull her up to your chest."

And so I did. I leaned forward, placed my trembling hands around her little arms, and pulled Adeline out of me, placing her gently onto my chest.

In that moment, time finally stood still. It was just me and my baby girl, our little *aloha* baby. We were both crying. Truth be told, the entire room was in tears at having just witnessed this event, but Adeline and I were in a world of our own, our chests lifting up and down in unison as we were finally united. Her skin was warm on my own, and I held her tightly to my chest knowing I would forever come back to this moment when I doubted my capability of doing this. She was mine and I was hers and we were in this, together.

"Would you like to cut her umbilical cord?" the doctor asked me, handing me the scissors.

"Yes," I said under my breath and in between sobs, thinking of how Brian had been the one to do so with both Izzy and Hudson. But he wasn't here anymore and now it was up to me.

Snip. Snip.

Just like that, for the first time in thirty-five weeks, Adeline and I had been separated, but we'd come closer in that moment than at any other point of our journey together. Cutting the umbilical cord was only the first of a lifetime of events that Adeline and I would have to experience on our own without him, but in this moment, I knew we could, we would do this.

We're in this together, sweet Adeline. We've got this.

Adeline Makai Bugge was born Tuesday, July 31, 2018, at 1:55 p.m., weighing six pounds, fifteen ounces.

Chapter Five

Bottle.
Swaddle.
Diaper change.
Nap.
Bottle.
Swaddle.
Diaper change.
Nap.
Bottle...wait, swaddle? Nap.

Adeline needs a nap. Hudson needs a snack. Izzy needs a bath. Hudson's cranky and probably needs a nap too. Izzy needs help with her sweatshirt, and now she wants a snack. Chance is barking and now the baby is awake.

This is miserable. I need help!

This was now my life as a solo parent to three children, all under the age of four. Describing our daily routine as chaotic would be an understatement.

"Huds—" *No, wait.* "Addy—" *Nope, wrong name again. Come onnn. Focus.* "Izzy! Put your shoes on, we have to go!"

"But Mama," Izzy said, hands on hips and furrowed brows, "I don't want to wear *these* ones!" she complained, pointing at the strappy brown sandals I recently bought for her, the ones she had chosen herself, the ones she had to have or she was going to have a meltdown right there in the middle of the store, the ones she apparently couldn't live without. The ones she was now refusing to put on.

"Isabel Blakely. I don't care, put them on." I hissed through shut teeth, holding two-week-old Addy in one arm, grabbing Hudson and his teddy bear with the other, and trying to balance myself while putting my own shoes on.

One, two, three kids? Check.

Toys for the car? Check.

Keys? Diaper bag? Snacks? Check.

And off we went, three screaming kids in the car, each one upset about something, my purse thrown on the empty passenger seat next to me, my uncombed hair tied up in a messy bun, my sweater already dotted with Adeline's baby spew she'd managed to get on me as we walked from the house to the car. And finally, the engine is on and the car is in drive.

I found myself lost in thought while driving through the streets of Boise, Idaho. Driving was my quiet time, the only time of the day I knew my kids were all OK, safely strapped in their car seats, and I could let my mind wander.

We were on our way to the grocery store, but I had taken the long route. I knew there were approximately seven stop lights between Nikki's house and the grocery store and if timed correctly with traffic, could give me twenty minutes of car time to feel sorry for myself and let myself cry without a house full of people having to witness it. I stopped at the red light long enough to close my eyes. Izzy and Hudson were now arguing with one another in the back seat, Adeline would need a bottle soon, and my patience was wearing thin. *This is hard. I miss Brian.* Tears rolled down my cheeks as I opened my eyes, blurring the red light ahead of me. I just needed to breathe. I'd been in survival mode the past few months, and today was no different, but sitting at this stop light with a car full of kids, in that very moment, I realized it had been months since I'd taken a deep breath.

I checked the rearview mirror, the light ahead of me—still red—and closed my eyes again. I inhaled. For a moment, I held it in. And released. *Whew, this feels good. I need to find a way to be OK. I will be OK. I've been a solo mom of three for two weeks already, I can do this.*

I opened my eyes, and I sensed the corners of my lips shyly turning upward. This was hard, but I could do it. I knew I would. I needed something to look forward to though, something to get excited about. The light turned green, and I continued driving, my mind beginning to consider the possibilities. *What would help me find my smile again? What would help me find my confidence? What would help show me I could in fact manage three kids and this new way of life on my own?*

That afternoon, home from the store and with the groceries put away, I couldn't put the kids down for a nap fast enough. Content with the fact I had about an hour of quiet time before I'd be back to mom duty, I walked into my makeshift bedroom and sunk down into the too-soft-for-me mattress and opened my laptop with more vigor than I had in a while, creating a brand-new Word document, and wrote in capital, bold letters:

TRIP TO AFRICA

I had thought about it the rest of the car ride home from the store. Sounds from the kids arguing unable to penetrate my thoughts this time, I knew I needed to plan a trip. Something exciting and extravagant enough to give me the confidence I needed while finding the balance in my new life as a solo parent. I needed something positive to think about and look forward to in moments of despair or when parenthood felt overwhelming. I could channel my energy into planning the trip of a lifetime, not only for me but also for my three children.

I leaned back, letting the feathered guest-room pillow support my back as I stared at those three words that excitedly bounced off of the sharp white screen of my computer. My heart felt tingly, a sensation I hadn't experienced in what now felt like a lifetime. I raised my arms and crossed them behind my head, suddenly realizing I could feel the sensation of my hair on my fingertips. For the first time in months, I was completely aware of myself and what was happening around me. I quickly and quietly felt the tears on my face, but they no longer tasted of anguish nor did they burn my skin with grief. These tears were different and were accompanied by a sense of accomplishment, of strength knowing I had the courage to get through this.

I closed my eyes, beginning to imagine the kids and myself in Africa, heading out on a safari for the day and hiking through uninhabited lands. I felt a sense of calm confidence creep back in and I knew in this moment that if I wanted to do it, I would make it happen and it would be amazing. And Brian would be so proud of me. Of us. *If only Brian were here witnessing me plan this, he would throw his hands in the air and shout "That's so cool, babe!"*

From: Brian
To: Ashley
Date: Sun, Jun 14, 2015 at 7:28 a.m.
Subject: RE: #23

Heya sweetheart! It's almost June 5th. You probably won't get this awhile though. The last email I got from you was dated the 25th of May. I think I could mail a letter to South Africa faster, haha! But it's better than nothing. I love you so much and I'm thinking of you all the time. I'm totally stoked for Australia! Seriously. I can't wait. Talk about the trip of a lifetime. It'll be so amazing. I want to see and do as much as we can, as long we get in some good diving days. I know there is a TON to do there though.

I can't wait to come home! OK babe, I gotta run. Please know that I'm thinking of you all the time and I love you so so so much. I can't wait to be home with you! Give everyone a giant hug and a kiss for me. ALLLLLLLLLL my love, always and forever!

<3 B

Brian and I had always shared a love of traveling. We enjoyed going on adventures together as well as on our own and had spent years of our lives traveling to destinations around the world. Brian had popped up in ports around the world with the Navy and been given the opportunity to explore each place a few days at a time, while I had saved every penny I ever made while working and put it into a special account which I'd tap only into once I had enough saved up to buy a plane ticket somewhere. I've stayed in seven-dollar-a-night hostels in Germany, I've found forty-dollar train tickets which allowed me to travel through Russia for a few days, a five-hundred dollar Groupon trip to China; I constantly scour discount travel websites looking for deals. I've never had a lot of money, but I have a deep desire to explore and find ways to make it work. From Australia and Mexico to Fiji and Portugal, Brian and I bonded over exploring the beauty the world has to offer, mingling with people we'd met along the way, enjoying learning about their cultures, soaking up their local knowledge, and appreciating their candor. Between the two of us, we've visited nearly fifty countries of the world; yet nothing had ever compared to the time we'd each spent in Africa. We had experienced something truly unique during our time there, a feeling hard to articulate, but one that left us longing for more. I wanted more of that feeling. I wanted my kids to experience that kind of feeling. I wanted to push myself and consume myself with thoughts of far-off lands and special adventures waiting to be had, especially understanding now more than ever that life can end as quickly as it begins. Planning a trip like this was something I knew I needed to do. For him. For me. For us. I had savings and years of experience traveling on a budget, and using some of the money we received after Brian's death, I treated this as a final gift from him to his children.

TRIP TO AFRICA

These words kept staring at me, demanding my attention back to the present. Yes, there was no doubt in my mind that Africa was going to be the best destination for us, so the kids would experience the same marvels that made Brian and me fall in love with the continent and its diverse culture and raw beauty.

As soon as I'd decided this was the perfect plan, doubts and insecurities began to creep in. *I'm adventurous, but am I crazy? It's hard enough going to the grocery store with all three kids...how am I going to make it to Africa on my own with all three in tow?*

Kayla! My thoughts were interrupted. Of course, I could ask Kayla, my recently hired nanny, if she wanted to come along on this trip. I began thinking of the best way to ask her. *Hey Kayla, I know you've only been working for me for a few days and we've only just met, but what are your thoughts on Africa? Wanna go?*

Nah, too awkward.

Hey Kayla, do you have plans for next summer? Because if you don't, perhaps you'd like to come on a trip to Africa with me and the kids?

Better.

I got up, walked out of my bedroom, and found Kayla in the kitchen, preparing herself a cup of coffee and enjoying the quiet that had settled in the house as all three children rested peacefully.

"Hey Kayla," I began. "I have a random question for you."

"Alright," she smiled. "What's up?"

"How would you feel about going to Africa next summer with me and the kids?" I didn't allow her time to answer as I continued on, hoping to give her more reasons to say yes, "I will of course pay for your entire trip since you'll be there to help me, and we can visit several countries!"

I could tell by her growing smile that I was about to receive a positive answer. The sparkle in her eyes told me she was just as excited as I was at the idea, but I kept going, more to myself than to her at that point.

"We could go on safaris, adventures," I continued, until it became too much for her to keep it all in and she exploded in a loud *YES!* followed by a contagious laugh. In the weeks preceding this moment, Kayla had heard tales of adventure and exploration my young family had already experienced, and she knew we typically brought a nanny or a friend with us to help with the kids on bigger trips, so she knew when the time was right, this way of life would make its way back to our family, and that she would likely be asked to travel with us. I felt my chest breathe a sigh of relief as a smile formed on my lips. My plan had been set in motion and I was going to make this happen. "I'm so happy," I told her, "we'll just have to get your vaccinat—"

Oh no!

In that moment, I realized during the past two hours I'd been formulating this idea, I had completely disregarded the fact that the kids would have to get special vaccinations to stay safe while traveling through Africa. Yellow fever, typhoid fever, malaria, hepatitis A and B—the list was growing in my head as I started thinking back to what I had needed on my previous travels.

Will Addy be old enough for those? She won't even be a year old yet...what about Izzy and Hudson? They're up to date on all of their vaccines, but that's a lot of new ones they'll need, and they're so young. I can't leave them behind. They need this trip as much as I do.

Standing in front of Kayla, whose coffee was growing cold, I began talking myself out of the trip I had just planned. "Let me think through this a little bit, but you'll need a passport... we're definitely going somewhere." I said with a smile. I excused myself, walked back down the hallway where I sat back down, and against my will clicked the backspace button on my keyboard:

TRIP TO

The cursor next to those two words kept blinking at me, insisting I fill the empty space with a new destination. Feeling pressured only by myself, I began searching my mind for a place I felt comfortable traveling to and that would not be too demanding on my children. I knew I needed and wanted this trip to be epic, extravagant, and filled with adventures—on the same scale as Africa would be. This trip would be a healing journey for the kids and me, building our confidence as a family of four to prove to ourselves we could do it, to show myself that I could raise these kids the way Brian and I had planned to, even though he wasn't here to be a part of it anymore. It also needed to be memorable and a tribute to Brian; to the family he had helped create. It was going to be a healing journey for me and the kids, an adventure that would make our bond even stronger and would allow us to embrace our new normal.

Memories of my own travels flashed through my thoughts like an old black-and-white movie. Trying times spent in South America in learning my grandma Isabel had died while I was hiking up Machu Picchu with my mom, chaotic times in Asia climbing my way to the top of the Great Wall of China, and then getting feverishly ill on my flight home, adventurous times in the South Pacific snorkeling our way through Australia and Fiji while pregnant with Hudson, and happy times in Europe exploring castles and ancient ruins as a family. I closed my eyes and thought of the countries Brian and I had visited together and separately, anxious to return home and recount adventures to one another and making plans to visit as a family one day. A memory of Brian's voice interrupted my thoughts as a map of Europe appeared on my computer screen, "I can't wait to take you and the kids to Norway, Ash. Besides the Oregon Coast, it's literally my favorite place on Earth. You're gonna love it!"

I closed my eyes and drew in my breath.

I looked at the blinking cursor one last time before grinning and letting out my breath, typing the six letters on my keyboard. This was it. I let my hands rest on the keyboard and felt myself sink into the soft mattress. I closed my eyes, silently giving myself the strength and courage to know I could do this, before I opened them again to see the bold capital letters in front of me:

TRIP TO EUROPE!

Chapter Six

"Kasey!" I shouted as my best friend answered her phone. I was nervous and excited and relieved that she'd picked up and cut right into it. "What are you doing next summer? Wanna spend three months in Europe? Kayla's coming, too, and I could really use the extra help with the kids, and I'd love to have you with me on this journey." I don't think I took a breath in between all those words, nor did I leave her a chance to greet me back.

Kasey exploded in hearty laughter, which was contagious, and I started laughing too. I wasn't sure how else to respond, it was a big ask and I was nervous. Kasey had moved to Portland, Oregon from Alaska ten years prior and worked at the Cheerful Bullpen sports bar across the street from my downtown apartment. I spent a lot of time at that bar, using their free Wi-Fi for schoolwork, and enjoying my twenties by means of cheap whiskey shots and their iconic $1.99 hangover breakfast. Kasey was almost always working when I went in, and after a few friendly conversations she told me she didn't know anyone in the city and asked if I'd be her friend. Her charming and candid demeanor was irresistible, and we've been nearly inseparable since then. She was the first person I called the day Brian proposed to me, and she held my hand as we watched Izzy's heartbeat flicker for the first time across the ultrasound screen while Brian was deployed. She's been present for all of my life's ups and downs over the last ten years and naturally was also one of the first people to learn of Brian's sudden death.

"Aww, Ash!" she finally said the moment I paused long enough for her to get a word in. This little phrase packed a big punch, and I could read between the lines. We both knew that if I was planning a trip like this it meant that I was slowly finding my way back to the person I was before tragedy consumed me; that I was once again becoming the woman Brian fell in love with and married; to the mother that had once made my children laugh and had the confidence to tackle anything. I would never be the same as before, but I was now willing to find the new version of me. The version of me that would invite my best friend on a three-month long trip across Europe.

"So?" I asked, but I didn't need to hear her answer. I knew it was a *yes*.

"YES, I'm coming on that trip with you!" *There it is.* I could sense through the phone lines her smile was as big as the one currently on my face. *We're doing it. This is crazy.*

"Alright, I will plan everything," I said. "But I think you should choose one country you'd like to visit too. I want this to be a healing journey for all of us. With everything you've been through in your life, I think you need it just as much as the kids and I do."

"Seriously," Kasey said in disbelief. "I don't know what to say Ash, thank you for the opportunity."

"Just tell me where you'd like to go!" I was chipper, happy she'd agreed to join us. This was the first time in months that I felt a sense of hope for happiness ahead. I'd been absolutely consumed with sadness since Brian's death, and even if this trip didn't materialize, the mere thought of it, and of finding a little bit of "normal" for our family gave me the spark I needed to continue. I knew this would be an experience we'd all remember forever. "Do you have any ideas off the top of your head?" I asked, already knowing what she'd say.

She took a deep breath and there was a moment of silence. I could picture her closing her eyes, imagining the place she'd talked about visiting for as long as I'd known her, a place dear to her heart and a part of her own story, but one she'd never taken the time to visit before.

"Ireland," she whispered into the receiver with a hint of hope that this trip would be the reason for her to finally visit the land her family had come from. In her young life, Kasey had suffered terrible losses, including the car crash that claimed the life of her mother when Kasey was only five, the accidental death of her brother at the age of seventeen, and the heart attack that took her father shortly after her twenty-seventh birthday. Kasey's brother, Johnny, had passed away in his sleep only a few years before I met her, and I knew Ireland was a place he'd dreamed of going and a place Kasey had desperately wanted to visit to pay tribute to him. She's lived through the unimaginable, planning and attending the funerals of her entire family, but had somehow come through it with a positive outlook and an unrivaled zest for life as she encourages others along the way. Kasey is an inspiration to me, and I knew she needed to be a part of this.

I smiled.

"Then Ireland it—"

"Oh!" Kasey suddenly interrupted me. "This is literally a dream come true for me, Ash, I'm going to cry!"

And just like that, travel plans were under way.

Three months. Three kids. Three adults. Three backpacks. The plan was coming along well. I had the kids, the traveling companions, and the will to make it happen. Now I just needed to select the countries to visit.

"Kayla," I said while she was sitting on the carpet, legs crossed, coloring with Hudson. "Is there a country you'd like to visit when we go to Europe?"

I must have caught her off guard because she looked at me with a puzzled expression as if to say, *Are you kidding me? I'm going on the trip of a lifetime and you want me to pick a country?!*

"Nope," she said, smiling at me. "I never even thought I'd leave the United States, so I'll be happy no matter where we go!"

"Alright then," I said, "I'm going to put Addy down for a nap and start planning in case you need me."

She smiled back.

Once the baby was asleep, I sat on my bed, lifted the laptop screen, and typed:

Google Flights

After checking a few flight scenarios, I realized that the cheapest flight to get us over to Europe would be from New York City to Amsterdam, The Netherlands. *Perfect!* I had never been to The Netherlands, but had always wanted to visit it.

Amsterdam. Check!

But where to go from there?

Google Maps

There were so many countries to pick from and my search quickly became overwhelming. I took a deep breath and leaned my head back when something from the corner of my eye caught my attention. It was a ray of sun streaming through the otherwise darkened room, shining on the frame next to my bed that held Brian's photo. I gently picked it up and returned his warm smile. *Look at that dimple.* I brought my trembling fingertips on my lips, kissed them, and gently placed them on the glass of the frame. I knew where we had to go next. *"I can't wait to go visit Norway with you, Ash. You're gonna love it!"*

Norway. Check!

One of the main criteria I used to decide which countries made the cut was the access we'd have to the ocean in each one of them. I've always found bodies of water—especially the ocean—to be healing and therapeutic, and I know it was the same for Brian…after all, the ocean was the background of nearly all of our favorite moments together.

***

"So, umm…I was thinking of going down to the Oregon coast on Friday night, just walking around Fort Stevens and hanging out for a little bit…" Brian said to me in an awkward conversation in June 2004. I'm pretty sure he was trying to ask me on our first date, but also knew he was incredibly shy and that if I wanted to make it happen I was going to have to invite myself.

"I love the coast, can I ride down with you if you go!?" I responded. He was relieved, and with that we'd cemented plans for our first date. Between childhood trips to the coast, flashbacks to a book my dad bought me when I was a kid about poisonous fish and other marine animals, a fascination with the unexplored, wanting to see what others didn't take the time to, and now this special first date with a handsome man…the ocean made me feel unique and special, and it's a feeling you can't explain to somebody; unless they feel it too.

***

Despite the circumstances that claimed Brian's life, the ocean makes me feel safe. It makes me feel content and whole, like I understand it and it understands me, and I needed to feel this in order to begin healing. On top of being an experience meant to bring healing to the kids and me, I also wanted this trip to be an educational opportunity for all of us, which meant planning out a few select destinations in each country. In Amsterdam, I wanted to visit Anne Frank's hiding place, a memorial that means so much to so many people and represents an important piece of world history. Despite the controversial decision to bring children here, next on the destination list was the Auschwitz concentration camp, in then German-occupied Poland to learn about the atrocities committed there. I knew these would be some very emotionally taxing destinations for all of us, and that we'd need to balance these out with a little more lighthearted fun in countries we'd seen pictures of but didn't know much about. From there I decided we'd spend some time unwinding in the Swiss Alps and then fly off to the white houses and blue domes made famous in photos of Greece. To conclude the trip, we'd have a pint of Guinness in the Emerald Isle and finally soak in the heated waters of the Blue Lagoon in Iceland!

Alright, that's The Netherlands, Norway, Poland, Switzerland, Greece, Ireland, and Iceland. Eight weeks. Seven countries. Six people.

We're doing it.

Planning this trip brought me back to life. As much as I love the experience and excitement of exploring new places, I've also always enjoyed the planning it takes to get us there. Working within the confines of a budget, kids sleep schedules, traveling only on the days I could find the cheapest plane tickets and accommodations, while utilizing reward points and frequent flier miles to make it possible. There was so much to consider while booking this trip, it consumed me, and also sparked in me a light that up until that moment, I'd felt had been washed away by the same waters that had taken Brian. Now, when I woke up in the mornings, the feeling of weight on my chest that had prevented air from reaching my lungs was slowly diminishing. I opened my computer screen each morning, looking at the trip plans I'd made the day prior and felt the slightest flicker of confidence running through my veins, that little flame that so dimly—yet desperately—was there to remind me that there was still life in me. Maybe, just maybe, I could get through this and somehow find a new normal.

What motivated me even more to keep planning the trip was knowing that Brian would have loved the idea. He would have been just as excited as I was to go visit all the countries with our three children. We talked endlessly about how important it was to allow our children to explore the world, to have them become acquainted with different cultures, to introduce them to new life-styles, and to let them experience the ways other people lived life. We truly believed travel, experience, and education were the best ways for our children to have open minds and welcome diversity—by teaching and showing them that the world is beautiful because of it.

This exact scenario also made planning this trip bittersweet. Brian wouldn't be with us. We wouldn't be taking pictures with him or making the memories we'd talked about making together in each of these destinations. We were taking this trip because of him, but he wasn't here. Everything had changed when Brian died, and I missed my life with him. I missed him. His presence, his smile, his embrace, his voice.

Suddenly, I felt an urge. I quickly picked up the phone, dialed his number, and called his phone.

"Hi, you've reached Brian. I'm sorry to have missed your call, please leave me a detailed voice message and I'll get back to you as soon as I can."

His voice. Oh, his voice. I miss this voice.

Tears.

Tears.
Tears.

October 17th*, 2018*
I called his cell phone tonight to hear his voice. I could hear how happy he was, picture his beautiful smile, and remember the way he articulated certain words. The way he said "Ambliance" instead of "Ambulance" and how I'd laugh at him every time—so much so that he just started doing it to make me give him that look, knowing it was coming. It's midnight on a Thursday night here in Boise. I'm exhausted but can't sleep. My Fitbit tells me I average two hours and thirty-six minutes of sleep a night—not bad for the stress from the past nearly five months of my life, but certainly not enough to make me feel like I'm capable of tackling much in the form of solo parenting. I'm going through the motions of being a mom, but I'm missing out on the joys of having a new-born, of watching Izzy and Hudson develop into toddlers and young children. I know I'll get back there at some point, but the reality of grief is that there is no timeline. Izzy and I looked at pictures of Brian on my laptop last night for nearly an hour. She kept asking to see photos of the two of them together and then would tell me where it was/what they were doing there. Later that night I came back down to my room to see her looking at the photos again but when I walked in, she started crying. Like a full-on meltdown sad cry. I asked her what was the matter, and she said she didn't want to tell me. I sat down

next to her and asked again. She crawled in my lap and kept saying she didn't want to tell me. I let her cry but continued to prod as to what was the matter. She finally told me "I miss Dadda. I thought he was going to come to Boise, but he's not." She said this a couple of times through her tears, saying she wanted him to come here and that she misses him. She said he can't come to Boise because he sank to the bottom of the ocean and she was sad. It was finally hitting her that he's not coming back.

Working on planning this trip also brought me to another realization: I didn't want to live in Boise, Idaho. Brian and I had never planned on living in, or raising our children in Idaho. However, at the time I made the decision to have Adeline here, it was what I needed to do for me and my children. The Pacific Northwest had always been home base: it was where Brian and I had originally met and fallen in love, where we'd brought home two of our three babies, and where we began to create our life together. I felt the strong call of the snowcapped mountains and mighty Pacific Ocean pulling me home. With each passing day, I was building my courage and confidence back up and part of this needed to include finding my independence again, in a new home, raising our kids as we'd intended, in a place that felt like home.

I shared the news with Nikki and Terry. They were sad to see us leave, but happy because they knew this meant I had a little fight in me after all and that I was ready to start moving forward. I began an extensive and exhausting house-hunting search online and was happy when I eventually found one I liked, within my budget and close to everything I needed. I immediately booked a round trip flight, and the next day, one-month-old Adeline and I boarded a twin-engine plane for the one-hour flight from Boise to Portland, Oregon, to check it out. My dad met us for the walk-through, and by the end of the day I'd submitted an offer. I flew back to Boise, found out the offer was accepted, and spent the next few weeks traveling back and forth for all of the house-buying inspections and meetings, with now two-month-old Addy by my side.

Time to move.

Again.

But this time we're headed home.

Well, our new version of home.

Moving day came and went. The navy sent a uniformed officer to help oversee the unloading of the giant wooden crates labeled "Bugge," each filled with contents of the life I'd shared with Brian, and which I hadn't seen since the morning we'd left Oahu. I knew being reunited with these things would be an emotional experience, and I wanted the house to be set up and made to feel like home before the kids saw it, so the kids stayed with Nikki while I made this journey on my own. On my flight over, I couldn't help but feel defeated in the fact I was returning to my hometown after all of this. Not because I didn't like it. On the contrary, I was happy they'd be able to experience some of the things I had when I was a child; searching for shells at the Oregon coast, sledding between the tall Evergreen trees up on Mt. Hood, weekend hiking in the Columbia River Gorge, and even more so that I had a place I considered safe and comfortable in which to raise them. This hadn't been my home for a number of years, and I didn't mind going back there to visit from time to time, stopping by for a cup of coffee to catch up with old friends, or marveling at the outline of Mt. Hood on our way through, but moving back as a widow with three children in tow? No. I just didn't want *that* to be the reason why I had to move back there.

Yet, here I was.

My friends put so much effort into helping me make our new house a home. They unwrapped boxed, arranged kitchen appliances, bought lunch, and gifted me with smiles and hugs in hopes of making me feel better. The kids and I had an entire community of support embracing us. When the day ended and all the boxes had been unpacked and empty crates placed back on the moving truck, my friends waved goodbye and went on about their lives, home to their own loved ones for the night. I stayed up late, arranging stuffed animals and books in the kids' rooms before settling in for a few hours of sleep on the floor of my new bedroom, exhausted and sad, but hopeful for all that was ahead for us as a family in this new house.

I couldn't sleep. I tossed and turned on the floor of my room, the overwhelming smell of fresh paint closing in on me. *Home.* I thought. "Home…" I whispered to the gray walls. This was it. I looked at the clock, counting down the hours until I'd be flying back to Boise to pick up the kids and bring them home with me. If I wasn't going to sleep, I might as well write.

With exhausted hands and trembling fingertips, I picked up my laptop and began writing:

People keep asking me if I'm excited to be buying this house. If I'm excited to be moving and back in Vancouver. While I do my best to put a smile on my face to get through the conversation without breaking down in tears, the real answer is no. Nothing about this is exciting or happy or good news. The real answer is deep and dark and depressing. The real answer is that in a matter of six minutes I went from sharing my life with my best friend to being a pregnant widow forced to make terrible decision after terrible decision. The real answer is that I don't want to do this. I want to be in our home in Hawaii, watching the kids play in the kiddie pool in our front yard. I want to be complaining that it's too hot while scratching mosquito bites and posting photos of giant cockroaches on Instagram. I want to get off our patio furniture at the sound of Brian's truck coming down the street and watch the kids run to the end of the driveway to hug him and watch him laugh—equally excited to see them after a long day at work. I know that's not the answer people expect to hear when they ask that question, but that's the truth.

This isn't exciting.

This is necessary.

Chapter Seven

*Y*ou'll move on. There wasn't a single expression I'd heard in the months preceding Brian's death that upset me more. *How could I possibly move on after losing my husband?*

I pushed it out of my head. In reality, I didn't want to think about it, and I didn't have time to think about it. Moving on? I was barely hanging on. I had three small children to raise and was too busy tending to their needs to worry about much else. I had two children in diapers, a newborn needing to eat every few hours, sibling squabbles to constantly break up, piles of toys to clean up, a dog to walk, and a house full of emotions to manage. I was responsible for a lot of living beings and it was exhausting.

"Mom! Hudson hit me!" Izzy screamed.

"No I didn't! Izzy bit me!" Hudson yelled back, tears running down his face.

Good grief. Somebody please hit me with something and knock me unconscious for just a few minutes of peace. "Both of you, knock it off or you're in big trouble!"

It was all up to me now. Brian and I had been more than husband and wife; we were partners in this parenting thing. We made every important decision together and shared the workload that came with managing a household and raising children. We both worked full-time and had hectic schedules, Brian was in the Navy, and I was a national training manager for a first-aid company, so we shared the responsibilities—and annoyances—that came with a houseful of young children. Kids unable to sleep? I might have to shake him awake, but Brian would get up in the middle of the night, grab his pillow and blanket, and sleep on the floor in their bedroom so they wouldn't feel alone or scared. He did it so I could get some rest. Kids too hyper on the weekend when I had work to get done? Brian would find fun adventures for them to go on so I could have some quiet time. Kids feeling sick? Brian and I would decide whether it was better to take them to the doctor right away or wait it out for a bit and see how their symptoms progressed.

But my life had changed drastically. I no longer had my partner to rely on, and this reality hit me like a ton of bricks one night when I felt very sick. Sharp pain in my lower abdomen, nausea, fever...I knew those symptoms all too well because I had suffered an erupted ovarian cyst before.

"Dad," I called the only person I could think of who lived close and could help me.

"Ashley?" He asked in a groggy voice filled with interrupted sleep. "Is everything OK? It's the middle of the night. Are the kids OK?"

The pain had progressed, my nausea had turned to full blown throwing up, and I needed help. Four-month-old Adeline awakened and needed a bottle, and I sobbed as I held her to my chest and threw up over the side of my bed. I told myself this had to be the lowest point of my new life as a solo parent. In this moment, I was desperate. "I need help, Dad." My dad and I haven't always had the closest relationship, but with few questions asked, he got in his bright blue pickup truck and drove the hour south to my house in the middle of the night, anti-nausea pills in hand, to help me. He spent the rest of his night in the bright red chair in my living room, holding, rocking, and feeding Adeline while I worked through the turmoil going on in my abdomen.

You'll move on. With Izzy in school and Hudson and Adeline spending their days going on grand adventures with Chandra, "Chananny," a dear friend who stepped up as a temporary nanny and who loved my kids as if they were her own, I had some free time each day to think through our upcoming trip to Europe. Slowly but surely, I came up with a loose plan. I decided that we would first go visit my little brother and his family who lived just outside of New York City and spend a week with them, catching up and letting the cousins play while we waited for Kasey to wrap up work in Portland and join us. From there, we'd head to the city famous for its red-light district, windmills, and canals that cut through the bicycle-lined city streets. From Amsterdam, we would then go to Oslo, Norway. This country was the main reason why I chose to embark on a European tour to begin with. Outside of the Oregon Coast, this was Brian's favorite place on Earth. The trees, the ocean, the boats, the laidback lifestyle... he loved it all. He was also successful in tracking down his family heritage there, all the way to the Bugge (authentically pronounced Bug-gay) café. He had been a few times with the navy on work trips and was anxious to bring me with him on the next one, hoping to dive the Norwegian Sea. Cold water diving wasn't my favorite, but he didn't mind one bit and was excited to add Norway to his diving résumé.

From Norway, we would then go to Warsaw, Poland. I have been fascinated by the history of World War II since high school and after reading about it for years, wanted to pay my respects to the lives lost at the Auschwitz concentration camp. I was also very cognizant that, although the children wouldn't remember much of this trip given their young age, one day I'd be able to show them photos of their visits to these important places and tell them stories of when we went there.

After Poland, we'd plan on traveling to Switzerland to hike the Swiss Alps, take in views of the Matterhorn and eat a whole lot of Swiss chocolate. Switzerland was the only country we'd be visiting that didn't have direct access to the ocean, which at some point along the way had become an integral part of our traveling plans, so from there we'd head to Greece. In Athens, we'd immerse ourselves in the delightful culture, nearby Aegean Sea and delicious food that included *spanakopita* (flaky phyllo pastry filled with hearty spinach and crumbled feta) fresh veggies, and baklava, the famed, nut-filled, honey-glazed phyllo pastry delicacy. My mouth watered at the thought of consuming gluttonous amounts of these treats as well as hummus and freshly made feta cheese before taking in sights of the Parthenon and Acropolis. From Athens, the six of us would hop a flight to Santorini, famous for its white-washed walls and blue rooftops and known to be one of the most beautiful islands in the world.

From there, we'd trade in the warm, bright blue waters of Greece for the cold, deep green sea that surrounded Ireland. Although Kasey had expressed her desire to visit the country, I was also very much looking forward to this stop. In 2010, I spent a week in Ireland on a backpacking trip with my little brother, Benny, and even with all of the traveling I've done since then, I've never experienced a place like it. Music flowing from the open doors of bars as you walk down the street, beautiful faces with lilting Irish accents offering *G'mornings*, the lush green countryside that reminded me of home, the feeling of vastness experienced while standing on the tall cliffs, staring out at the open ocean. "I could live there!" I told Benny upon our return home from that trip. It's a stunning place, one of the most beautiful in the world.

From Ireland, we would reach our final stop in Reykjavik, Iceland. This country wasn't new to me. In 2011, I spent a week there by myself, knowing nothing of the country or what to expect, yet delighted with how beautiful it was. I knew I'd return someday, which is what I did in 2017, this time with Izzy and Hudson in tow, witnessing the same sights and sounds I experienced six years earlier as a single traveler, but now getting to share it with my two children. It was incredible. Iceland would be an important and emotional leg of this trip, and a great way to wrap up our summer adventure. I've spent time in this country during incredibly different stages of my life: as a single woman, as a wife and mom of two out for a fun adventure with her kids, and now a widow with three young children in tow. I knew I wanted to retrace my own steps on the island, and I hoped to return there for a moment of healing.

As exciting and therapeutic as it was to plan this trip—from booking flights to making Airbnb reservations—the reason behind the need for this trip was always prevalent and Brian was never far from my thoughts.

You'll move on. The meaning escaped me. How could I possibly move on from the grief that I still carried around with me? At times, the sadness became unbearable and all I could do was cry. I typically retreated to the bedroom closet of my new home in moments like these, the four walls and solid wooden door offering a temporary protection to and from my kids whom I wanted to shelter and shield from having to witness their mom breaking down. Nestled between sweatshirts bearing the names of places Brian and I had traveled and explored together, I'd sit on the floor with my head between my hands and let it out. The sadness, the frustration, the feelings of pity I had for myself, for a brief moment would wash away with the tears streaming down my face. "Mama?" Izzy found me. "Hudson took my purple marker and I told him 'that's not nice' but he did it anyway!" With that, my moment would be over, the needs of my four-year-old daughter and getting to the bottom of this purple marker debacle taking precedent. In the months following, I spent less time crying in the closet, and more sharing the emotional moments with the kids. I wanted to teach them that it was OK to show emotion and be sad in front of one another, to get through the hard moments together, to lean on each other as a family, and the only way to do that was to lead by example.

Between caring for three children, planning our upcoming travels, and trying to document it all, I looked at the calendar and realized that somehow months had gone by since I had moved back to the Pacific Northwest. Winter had turned to spring, Izzy's school year was coming to an end, Hudson's bear was still attached to his hip—some things never change— and Addy was no longer a newborn but had graduated to the title of infant.

How is it March already? I was standing in the kitchen packing Izzy's school lunch and thinking through my plans for the day; *get Izzy to school, Hudson's dentist appointment at 10:00 a.m., go to the post office, call Addy's pediatrician about missing her one-year visit while we're overseas, start packing list, find someone to watch Chance while we're gone, someone to mow the lawn while we're gone.* My thoughts were inter- rupted by the sound of Chance barking at the approaching mail truck outside. *Shoot! I forgot to check the mail yesterday.* I had a stack of "thank you" cards to send out anyway, so I put my shoes on, opened the door, and walked down the street to greet the mailman.

My mailman smiled back as we exchanged piles of mail and pleasantries. I thanked him and absentmindedly began looking through the stack he had handed me. *Bill, ads, coupons, Legacy of Life Hawaii*—the company who had facilitated Brian's organ donation. The ones who called me eight hours after Brian's death, who had asked for permission to harvest his organs and tissue in order to provide life, or a better quality of life, to others in dire need. It had been Brian's final wish, and as painful as the phone call was, it was one I'm humbled and proud to have had on his behalf. I received letters from the company a handful of times during the months prior, offering condolences to my family, so it was not uncommon to see their return address in a stack of my mail, but this letter appeared different. My pace slowed down as I walked back into the house and opened the envelope. Inside the large envelope, was another envelope. White, legal sized and sealed closed. *Weird.* I turned it around and in handwriting I didn't recognize; "From your grateful recipient" was scribbled across the front.

My heart dropped. The blood drained from my face and the bright red chair in my living room caught me.

Oh no.

In less time than it took for my heart to pump one more ounce of blood through my body, my thoughts flashed back to that phone call. To me, eight hours after kissing my husband's cold lips goodbye in the quiet room of the emergency department, sitting outside of our dark brown house in Hawaii, the palm trees swaying in the wind across the street, crying tears of pure anguish as I consented to my husband's body parts being distributed to potential recipients across the United States. And here it was, in my hands, a handwritten letter from one of the people he had physically been distributed to. My hands shook and I was crying before I even started reading the letter from Alissa, the forty-two-year-old single mother of three who tore her ACL in a terrible skiing accident. In perfect penmanship, she wrote of how she'd been a competitive runner her entire life, running marathons and half-marathons around the United States as a hobby of hers and was crushed when she thought she'd never be able to fulfill this passion again. How she could now, because of my loved one, be able to continue chasing after her children, ski, run, and live her best life. I wept as she wrote how sorry she was for the fact that she understood that her receiving this donation meant that we lost a loved one and how tragically sorry she was for our loss.

I finished the letter, set it on the counter, and let the tears run down my face. Even in death, Brian was still somehow motivating people to pursue their passions. His selfless gift of deciding to be an organ donor was having real effects on real people, and I had the letter to prove that he was continuing to change lives even after his own had ended.

It took me days to fully grasp the magnitude of what that letter had done for me, and for Brian, mostly because I had to sort through many conflicting emotions: I was proud of Brian for choosing to be an organ donor, yet I was painfully grieving his loss; I wanted nothing more than to have my husband back, but I found solace in this woman's words, knowing a part of him is living on through her. This was a beautiful, calming gift of knowledge and I knew immediately I would write her back.

March 19, 2018

Hi Alissa,

My name is Ashley, and I just received a letter from you that I was dreading yet hoping I'd someday receive. You were the recipient of my husband's Achilles tendon that replaced your own. I've never done this before, so I find myself at a bit of a loss for words and I truly don't know where to start this letter, so let me start here.

I can only imagine the courage it took you to write that letter. I've never had to write a letter to somebody thanking them for a literal piece of their loved one who recently died, so I can't say I understand how hard that must have been, but I can say I felt in your words how humbled you've been by the gift my husband, Brian, has given to you. I've read through it at least a dozen times, experiencing sweeping emotions in every possible direction as I do, but I can tell you with certainty, your words and this letter are something I will cherish forever.

I appreciate you telling me about yourself, your circumstances, and letting me see firsthand that Brian's wish of being an organ donor has been granted. This knowledge is not something everybody gets, and I can't express how grateful I am to know those hard conversations he and I had come down to this moment, this letter, and I know he would be so incredibly proud to see this is as the result.

Brian. My husband. My children's father. A son, a brother, a friend. A Naval officer. A sailor. A scuba diver. An adventurer. This is a slight glimpse of the man whose tissue now resides in your knee. You should know that tendon enabled my 35-year-old husband to have more adventures and see more of the world than most see in their entire lives. He traveled around the world countless times, sailed our 36' boat across the Pacific Ocean, scuba-dived in countless reaches of the world, ran marathons (yes, he was also a marathon runner!) and most importantly, helped raise two of our three beautiful babies with me. Brian took advantage of every single day of his life, with a motto of "no bucket list!" Do it now, because you never know if tomorrow will come. Unfortunately for all of us, that day came much too soon for him, but knowing this small part of him will continue to live on in you helps me believe he'll get to keep exploring and having grand adventures.

I was six months' pregnant with our third child, Adeline, when Brian passed away, and we also had a one-year-old (Hudson) and a three-year-old (Isabel) at home so he only got to experience being a dad to our first two, but I see so much of his adventurous, kind, and loving spirit in each of our kids.

I now know firsthand what it feels like to be a single mom to three children, and how important our health and ability to chase after them is. I'm thankful this part of him went to you to enable you to be this and do this for your family. I sincerely hope we're able to continue communication, if you're up for it, I'd love to get to know you and see some of Brian's dreams realized through you.

Also, sorry for the typed—instead of handwritten letter— my handwriting is TERRIBLE, and you'd have a hard time reading it. ☺

Thank you again for your kind letter, you don't know how much I appreciate it.

I hope to hear from you soon.

After I was done writing it, I looked outside my living room window, staring at nothing but everything at the same time. I began thinking of everything I'd been through, the decisions I'd had to make, the many ups and downs I'd faced since Brian's death, and the variety of experiences that had come with—and because of—each of those decisions. This letter had changed things for me, and I knew in this moment that while I was not ready to move on, I was ready to move *forward.*

Chapter Eight

I would never dive again; I was certain of it. The thought of pulling on my fins and mask and looking out at the horizon as I took a giant stride off the back of a dive boat— it was too much. I was spooked. The incredible memories of swimming among manta rays, sharks, and sea turtles, were life-changing experiences and would now be a thing of the past that I had to be OK with. Brian and I had taken our very first breaths underwater in November 2014 during a "Discover Scuba Diving" course he'd surprised me with in Hawaii. We were briefed by our instructor and before we knew it, the boat had grabbed its mooring ball, our air tanks were turned on, we were tapping the tops of our heads indicating we were OK, and just like that, our first splash as our fins hit the water. We spent the next hour exploring an area off the coast of Waikiki known as "The Pipe" looking for sea turtles, octopuses, and *humuhumunukunukupua'a* (the Hawaiian state fish.) It had taken only that single breath, the sight of a thousand tiny bubbles escaping our lips by means of the regulators attached to our mouths to know our lives would be forever changed.

"That was INSANE!" Brian had exclaimed as we surfaced from that very first dive.

"That was amazing!! We have to get certified!" I shouted back, the wind and waves pelting me in the face as we made our surface swim over to the boat ladder.

We'd go on to dive in waters around the world, from Mexico to Fiji, from Australia to our backyard in the Puget Sound, but we never forgot that very first dive in Hawaii and how those warm tropical waters had changed everything for us. This would unfortunately be the devastating reality for us as it was these exact tropical waters of Hawaii where Brian would take his final breath in May 2018. So, as much as scuba diving had been a part of our lives for years, as much as I love the ocean and the experiences that I'd had in it, I loved my three children more. *If I don't dive, I can't die in a diving accident.*

"Are you going to dive with us?" One of Brian's friends asked as I began making arrangements to return to Hawaii for the one-year anniversary of his death. "No, I don't think I can." The deep sadness and regret apparent in my voice. It had been a year. An entire year since that phone call, since seeing him for the last time, hearing his voice, feeling his touch. An entire year. The first half of that year had been consumed with moving, giving birth to Adeline, moving again, and trying to figure out what I was doing, while the most recent months had been spent planning a proper memorial and subsequent memorial scuba dive in honor of Brian.

Plans began to take shape and soon I had a team of twelve divers flying in from around the United States who wanted to be a part of this memorial dive with the opportunity to say goodbye to their dive buddy and one of their own. During the early stages of planning, Living Reef Memorial graciously offered the gift of a reef for Brian and our family. The owner explained he'd use a combination of Brian's cremains and organic materials to create a reef that would be lowered to the ocean floor. This reef would become a part of the local ecosystem—in essence returning Brian to the ocean he so loved while it also created an environment for local animals and sea life to thrive in. First up, I needed to get some of Brian's ashes to San Diego where the company was headquartered in order to make the reef. "How much/how many do you need?" was one of my first questions to the director. *A measuring cup worth? An arm's worth?* These morbid thoughts swirled through my head as I began planning, but this was unprecedented and certainly nothing I'd ever had to work through or speak about before. "How do I know how much of Brian to part with?" I asked in the calmest way I could muster. When I received the response, "As much or as little as you'd like, we can work with whatever you're comfortable sending," I knew I wasn't the first person to have asked that question and I felt better. Brian and I had discussed our final wishes with each other, and I knew when he died, he wanted to be scattered at sea, but I also knew that if he'd known about this as an option, he would have chosen this in a heartbeat, so I graciously accepted the gift, parted with some of his ashes, and began making plans.

It took months and a lot of help to plan it all; coordinating schedules, divers, boats, and shipment of the two-hundred-pound reef to the island, working with press outlets; and finally, leaving the home we were building in the Pacific Northwest for the home we'd left in Hawaii. This was a huge emotional undertaking to put all of these plans in place, knowing I'd be stepping foot back on the island and watching from a boat as his friends placed "Brian" back into the ocean. I thought about it again and soon decided there was no way I could just watch from the boat as this happened. I had to be in the water. I had to see with my own eyes as he was returned to the ocean floor. I had to see his final resting place, I had to feel it, to be a part of it, just as he'd been a part of me.

"I'm doing the dive," I told Eric, one of Brian's friends and a diver stationed on the island who'd been instrumental in helping me pull it all put together. Eric worked with Brian at the U.S. Pacific Fleet headquarters at Pearl Harbor, and they'd bonded over their love of diving, sailing and all things blue-water related. Eric had been instrumental in helping me put plans together for this memorial dive; arranging dive boats and coordinating schedules and flight times of the dive team traveling to the island for the event.

"You are?!" Shock registered in his voice. "You don't have to. You know that, right? We'll take good care of him, Ash," Eric said cautiously, appreciating what a difficult decision this was for me to make, but also understanding the desire for me to be in the water with Brian's reef. The truth is, I knew it would be excruciating, I knew jumping into that water with my dive gear on would be one of the hardest things I'd ever do, but I also knew if I didn't do the dive, I'd regret it. I'd regret that fear had taken precedence over the opportunity to do this, to which there'd be no second opportunity. This was my one chance to be a part of his memorial dive, to say goodbye to him in the same waters where we fell in love with diving, to see with my own eyes what he'd seen the last few moments of his life, to be there for him as I knew he'd do for me if the circumstances were reversed. I had to do it. There was no other option. I explained my decision to Eric and the other divers on the team, and knew this would create an additional element of emotion in a highly emotional situation. I wanted to give them the opportunity to withdrawal from the dive if they weren't comfortable with it. The opposite reaction was had by all, who responded with messages like, "You've got bigger balls than me, girl! I'm so friggin' proud of you!" and "We'll look out for you, Ash. I'll personally hold your hand the entire dive and make sure you make it home to your kids." And, "Brian would expect nothing less, you're making him so proud."

The memorial dive was planned for May 19, 2019—364 days after Brian was pronounced dead in the Honolulu emergency room. As a group, we'd first dive the Sea Tiger, a shipwreck-turned-artificial-reef off the coast of Oahu and the same dive Brian was on the morning he drowned. Ninety feet under the ocean surface, we'd place an American flag on the stern of the wreck from the flag line and then each take our time diving the wreck, depositing seashells filled with his ashes that I'd prepared for each of the divers as a way to say their own goodbyes. Then we'd surface, let our bodies release the nitrogen being stored from diving, regroup, recover, recharge, debrief as a team, and then take the boat to the next dive site where we'd place his reef memorial.

A few days before the kids and I were scheduled to leave for Hawaii, I received a photo of the reef, draped with an American flag, and a message from the director that read: "Below are some photos of your husband's reef ready for pickup. We are all waiting for the driver. There are a number of vets here standing guard with him until he is taken away."

I felt incredibly proud and overwhelmingly sick at the same time. I could see the twinkle in Brian's eyes and hear his voice excitedly exclaiming, "Ash, this is so cool!" at the sight of the reef, but I also knew that I was looking at my husband's last form. Tears quickly and quietly fell from my eyes and rolled past my trembling lips, leaving me with the bitter taste of mourning. I'd been so consumed with the physical act of planning that I hadn't taken any time recently to think about *why* I was planning all of this. Seeing his reef draped with the American flag and thinking about a group of military veterans standing around it was too much, and the emotion of the moment took over.

I spent the days prior to our departure distracted with packing and figuring out last-minute details, and before I knew it, the distractions had all been resolved, plans were in place, and we'd be flying out in the morning on a plane bound for Hawaii. The house was quiet, all three kids were tucked into bed, and I had nothing left to do but confront the feelings consuming my thoughts. I wasn't ready to go back.

May 14th, 2019
Our flight to Oahu leaves at 10:30 a.m. tomorrow and I'm terrified at the thought of getting on it. I don't want to. I don't want to go back to the island. I don't want to

confront the sadness or the piece of my heart I left there. I don't want to get off the airplane and feel the humid Hawaiian air hit my face. I don't want to think of landing there on August 10, 2017, full of hope and excitement knowing this was going to be our home for the next three years. I don't want to think of Brian's dive locker setup in our garage. I don't want to think of our afternoons spent at Dog Beach, or the time Brian and Izzy both got stung by jellyfish at Bellow's. I don't want to think about the last photo taken of Izzy, Hudson, and me, pregnant with Adeline as we prepared to leave the island, heartbroken and bound for Boise on June 28, 2018. We didn't even make it a full year. I don't want to drive past our house, I don't want to close my eyes and see his smile because then I'll hear his laugh and my heart will somehow break a little bit more. I just don't want to. I don't want it to have been a year. I don't want to never see him again. I don't want his kids to not wrap their arms around him and laugh or cry. I don't want to see the excitement in everyone's eyes upon landing in paradise, while tears well up in my own. I don't want to know this has been real.

But it has. And I'm going to.

A few days later, I donned my diving kit, fins, and mask, and looked out at the horizon. I took a giant stride off the back of the boat and dove. I dove and I cried. I let it all out and said "goodbye." I watched as his friends and seasoned dive buddies did the same. With the hot Hawaiian sun shining on us, we dove down to the white sands of the ocean floor and swam past a school of butterfly fish and a lone sea turtle basking in the sunrays that illuminated the underwater world around us. These sea beings were apparently unphased by our presence or by the circle of bubbles that escaped from our regulators as we worked to lower Brian's reef into place. Brian's military brethren saluted his memorial and paid their respects to a fallen sailor and friend who'd lost his life doing something that was such a part of each of us. I've never felt more a part of something than I did on those two dives where we each savored the experience of being there, knowing this moment would stay with us forever. Eric and Adrian were true to their word and didn't leave my side the entire time, save for the few moments where we each placed our shells containing Brian's ashes on the Sea Tiger, and then came back together hand in hand to finish the dive.

Eric, Adrian, and I were the last to surface from the Sea Tiger dive. We grabbed the American flag from the stern upon our ascent. I held it tightly in my hands as I broke the surface and took the regulator from my mouth to take a big gulp of fresh air. I held that flag over my head victoriously. *I did it.* I knew I could, and once I'd made up my mind, I knew I would, but nothing could compare to the feeling of actually having done it. Fresh tears streamed from my eyes as the incredible team of divers surrounding me clapped, whistled, and cheered from their positions in the water. The tears kept on coming as I looked up and saw the familiar yellow hull of *Stay Gold*, the 36' sailboat Brian and I purchased in 2016 and that he had sailed across the ocean during our move to Hawaii in 2017. She had a new owner now, and thankfully and graciously that new owner had agreed to bring Izzy, Hudson, Addy, and the rest of our family and friends to witness us dive and place the memorial so they could all say their own goodbyes.

I pulled myself hand over hand along the tag line attached to the boat, and my body swished and swooshed with the ocean waves as I made my way to the back. I took my place in line amongst the dive team to climb the ladder, handed up my fins, took one final salt water filled breath before boarding the boat. The twelve of us each had tears in our eyes but smiles on our faces as we hugged and mourned and celebrated. *We did it.* We put Brian to rest in the most fitting way possible, and if he couldn't be here with us, we were proud to know he was exactly where he'd want to be. I grabbed the purple *lei* I'd brought onboard, and sat on the edge of the boat with my legs dangling in the water.

I pressed the fragrant flowers to my lips, kissed it goodbye, whispered *a hui hou* my love, and let it go.

Chapter Nine

"**M**y list!" I yelled to myself while pulling my car out of the driveway. I was on my way to the store to grab a few things I knew I wouldn't be able to find—or be comfortable buying—overseas, and I had forgotten my list on the kitchen counter. Exhausted from the effort before even making it to the store, I pulled the car back into my driveway, ran inside, grabbed the scrap of paper scribbled with things like *children's Tylenol* and *formula for Addy*, and quickly ran back out. With my car in drive and now-crumpled list in the seat next to me, I headed out.

I had been planning this upcoming European adventure for months. I'm not much of a planner by nature when it comes to travel, instead preferring to find flights and accommodations and then figure out the rest upon reaching my destination, but this trip was different. With three kids and two other adults in tow— all of whom I'd be responsible for—I tried to think through the potential of every possible scenario; kids getting sick, Hudson potty-training, Isabel's fifth birthday and Adeline's first, cribs and car seats and transportation arrangements for each of the kids, scheduling flights around nap times, Addy's potential first steps, and navigating multiple time zones and climates. There was a lot to think through and just as I had hoped for and needed, planning had consumed me.

What am I forgetting? The question nagged at me even more as I heard my own voice in my head. *Shoes for Addy in case she starts walking, small toys for the kids to open on long flights, a first aid kit and thermometer, travel converter/adapter, diapers, long pants for Iceland, bathing suits for Greece, birthday presents for Izzy and Ad...*my thoughts were suddenly interrupted by the here and now of my growing "to do" list—

"Cake!" It happened again. I suddenly realized that Izzy was going to celebrate her birthday abroad and was now old enough to expect a birthday cake! But I couldn't bring one with me, so I needed to add this to the list of things to figure out prior to departure. *Let's see, where will we be when she turns five?* Standing in front of a selection of travel body wash bottles in Target, I closed my eyes and tried following the lines of our imaginary itinerary. I was sure that by then we'd be out of Poland, but was it before Greece? I made a mental note to check the actual calendar and itinerary when I got back home. *All I need to do is remember I made this mental note.*

That was an expensive trip to Target. I won't give you exact numbers, but I will say if there was an award to be won for spending money on a seemingly random assortment of odds and ends at Target that day, you're looking at the gold star winner. I had enough children's Tylenol, baby formula and granola bars, along with whatever else ended up in my cart to last us through the next two months. The hard part would be finding room for it all in the three backpacks we'd be bringing with us.

"You're crazy! I could never do what you're doing." I heard time and time again. "I just don't understand why you're doing this." I heard from my own family. "What is the message you're trying to send here?" I heard from the media following my story. We'd be embarking on this journey in a few short days, and I had done my best to explain the *how* I was doing this to people, but I knew many were still grasping to understand the *why*.

"Ashley, I worry you're putting too much on your plate. Don't you want to take some time to settle down before doing something like this?"

"No, I don't. This journey is for us to heal, to bring us together and to make new memories as a family of four."

"Ashley, I've heard it's not very safe over there, what if—"

"No need to worry about the *what ifs*. We'll deal with them as they happen and be stronger for figuring it out together. That is, in essence, the entire premise of this trip. Figuring this all out together, as a family. The safety of my kids and travel companions is my highest priority, and we won't be doing anything that would jeopardize that."

"Ashley, I worry that perhaps visiting Auschwitz isn't the best idea after suffering such traumatic loss, not just for you but especially for the kids."

"This entire trip, and in part our visit to Auschwitz is all part of this healing journey we're on as a family. We have suffered loss this year, but we're not alone in that and this is an excellent opportunity for us to discuss loss across the board and what it looks like and feels like for others as well. Visiting a place of such historical significance where humankind suffered one of its greatest atrocities will no doubt be devastating but is also a gift of education I can give my kids, and an important one to me."

While I did have a few naysayers who just couldn't wrap their heads around the fact I'd bring my kids on a trip like this, for the most part, everybody was incredibly supportive and encouraging and excited to follow along and live vicariously through us. *I am a seasoned traveler, my children are well-traveled, I have two incredible traveling companions who I know will step up and help make this a great experience for all of us and I'm ready to do it.*

The days and hours prior to take-off were starting to wind down, but I still had a few loose ends to tie up before we set out.

Put mail on hold. Check.

Make copies of passports and itinerary for family. Check.

Let bank know I'd be traveling and to not block credit cards. Check.

Double check cell phone plan will work overseas. Check.

There was one more thing I told myself I was supposed to remember to do. I tried hard to remember what it was, but I couldn't. *Oh crap, I know I told myself to make a mental note of something...*

"Cake!" I yelled out to no one—again. "Izzy's cake." Between all of the other things going through my head at the time, I was proud of myself for remembering.

Alright, let's see...where will we be for Izzy's birthday? I sat down in front of my laptop, lifted the screen up, and opened the document titled Europe 2019. *Netherlands, Norway, Poland, Switzerland*...July 21 we'd be in Switzerland! *So fun!* This would be a busy stop for us as we'd be traveling through the country from Zürich to Zermatt, with a few stops in between, but my first born would only get one chance to celebrate her fifth birthday and I wanted it to be special for her. I knew that she wouldn't necessarily be able to understand how exciting celebrating a birthday in Switzerland would be, and how special of a day this truly was, but I also knew that twenty years from now, she'd look at the photos and smile at them. I wanted her to have that memory forever, so I was going to give her the best birthday I could, given our circumstances, and my limited ability to bring many birthday supplies with us. *OK, how do I get a birthday cake and party supplies to a remote farmhouse in Switzerl—*

"Addy's swim diaper!" I said, pointing my index finger up as if to make it a point to not forget, my mind quickly changing directions—again—as I added this to the ever-growing list of things I couldn't forget. The birthday cake arrangements would have to wait.

Coordinating schedules, creating packing lists, planning, answering questions, and running errands had filled my days since returning home from Brian's memorial dive in Hawaii and, before I knew it, we were thirty-six hours away from beginning our "No-Bucket-List" trip across Europe. After the children finally went to sleep, I took a moment to myself to think about Brian and the real reason for this trip. I couldn't believe where we were, how we got there, and what we'd been through. And now, here we were, nearly a year later, about to take off.

Eleven flights. Seven countries. Three adults. Three children. Three backpacks. Three car seats. A whole lot of coordination. People kept reaching out to me, wishing me good luck and safe travels, but they were also curious as to how I had made it all happen. Travel like this, especially with three small children, isn't common in the United States, and people were very interested in the details of how it would all work.

Can't sleep anyway, might as well try to answer some of their questions. So, I got up from my bed, walked to my faithful laptop whose keyboard had translated so many emotions into words over the past year, and began typing my latest blog entry:

June 18th, 2019

Wheels up in thirty-six hours! I should be packing, checking things off my to-do list, making sure I'm as prepared as can be for these next two months, however, I'm more of a last-minute-thrive-in-chaos kind of girl, so instead, I'm going to spend this time answering some of your most commonly asked questions about our upcoming trip!

Are you ready for your trip? *Ready? No. Prepared? Almost. I'm trying to remember to do things like set up auto billing for everything, find care for my dog, purchase what I need, get laundry done, coordinate flights and visits with friends, make lists of things I can't forget. I've got my backpack out on the floor near my bed and a couple of piles of things around it ready to be put in there. Kayla flies in tomorrow and then it's go-time. So, prepared? Almost. Ready, no. I wish I had another month, maybe two to get ready, just to emotionally acknowledge that the time is here.*

Did you plan this all yourself or are you going with a group? *I've planned every detail of this trip under the advisement of Isabel, Hudson, Adeline, and my two travel companions Kasey and Kayla and without trained professionals. Planning the countries to visit, flights, accommodations, and travel is exactly what I needed as a way to focus my energy on something positive.*

Where are you going? *Our first stop is going to be New York City for a couple of days to visit my little brother and a couple of friends and wait for Kasey to meet up with us. We then fly from NYC to Europe. We'll have a rental car in the majority of these countries so plan on doing some traveling around and through each of these countries pretty extensively to see what they have to offer!*

Are you nervous to travel with the kids? *No. Not one bit. I've been traveling internationally with the kids since Hudson was three months old. Brian and I took the kids to Portugal when Hudson was three months old and Izzy was two years old. They've been to five countries outside of the United States since then and have traveled through our own country quite extensively. They're expert travelers and I'm confident they'll do just fine. I've found as long as you are adequately prepared with plenty of snacks and (new) toys, they'll keep themselves entertained on the airplane, and we've got enough time built into each country that we're visiting, that if we need a day or two of downtime to just sit around the Airbnb/hotel, we'll have it without feeling pressure to go see everything right now. This will be Adeline's first international trip and she's got big shoes to fill in order to keep up with her brother and sister!*

How will you get around? Planes. Trains. Automobiles. We've got rental cars in all countries except for The Netherlands—I tried but they didn't have a car with automatic transmission that was large enough to fit us all, and I can't drive a manual! We'll utilize the metro and walking as much as possible but use our rental cars to travel outside the city centers when we want to. We'll fly from each country to the next to save time and to get to our destination a little quicker than we would if we traveled by rail.

What are you bringing with you? Thinking about this has consumed nearly as much time as planning the entire trip. Kasey, Kayla, and I each have a travel backpack. In it will be our own clothes and items, as well as one child's. We've each claimed a child at this point—Kayla/Izzy, Kasey/Hudson, and Me/Adeline. Because of the limited space we'll have to carry all of our goods, we've had countless group chats discussing who is bringing what so that we don't double up on certain things. Kayla's bringing the hair straightener. Kasey's bringing the curling iron and eyebrow tint. I'm bringing my laptop so we can all watch movies at night. We'll go to the market in each country upon arrival to buy necessities so we don't have to carry them from country to country. I've purchased and packed enough baby formula to (hopefully) make it through the entire trip as I remember we ran out in Portugal and it was a nightmare trying to find baby formula that didn't upset Hudson's belly at the time, so this time I'm prepared. I'll buy diapers and wipes in each destination country. I've packed Band-Aids and children's Tylenol, Advil, hand sanitizer, and nail clippers...Things that might be hard to find to somebody who doesn't know their way around *town and items I want to have on hand because of the kids. We're packing ten days' worth of clothing each, which should last us just about through each country, and nearly all accommodations we're staying at have washing machines, so we'll be able to do laundry consistently.*

Whew. Seeing the itinerary and the Q&A in my own words gave me this incredible feeling of relief and pride. I did it...at least on paper, I planned a two-month-long trip across Europe for the six of us and we would depart in the morning. The distractions associated with planning this expedition were exactly what I needed to pull myself through my depression; seeing this trip through would be the confidence boost I needed to know the kids and I would make it. Together as a family, this was it, this was us, and I'd come to realize that it didn't have to end just because Brian wasn't here to experience it with us anymore. He would forever be a part of our family, and the one who had instilled and encouraged this mentality of "No-Bucket-List:" do what you need to today, because tomorrow isn't guaranteed for any of us. This was our one life to live, and we would live it on our own terms.

A yawn reminded me it was time to go to sleep and try to get some rest. After all, I had a big trip to get ready for.

Chapter Ten

"We're doing it..." I whispered to myself as our plane began the descent into New York City. Known by people around the world as the city that never sleeps, NYC is home to Lady Liberty, New York style foldable thin-crust pizza, and the home base for countless television dramas and sitcoms, but it is known to me for apartment 407 in Williamsburg, Brooklyn—a fourth-floor walk-up loft I called home for a brief period of time in the mid-2000s. Our plane tipped its wing, and I could see the iconic skyscrapers hugging the Hudson River from my window seat, and the verdant green swath of Central Park just to the north as it stood out amongst the monotone gray of the rest of the city. We were close now and I could picture the buzzing metropolis below us, yellow taxi cabs zipping down Broadway, the blinding billboards of Times Square, the rumbling of the L train heard while walking through Union Square and the smells of Indian and Italian food seeping from hole-in-the-wall restaurants sprinkled throughout the city.

I pictured the hordes of people below us navigating streets filled with vendors and performers, wearing suit jackets and sequin dresses as they headed uptown to a Broadway show or donning ripped jeans and flannels in the lower East side as they walked into dimly lit pubs for an overpriced glass of whiskey and a night out with friends. I heard the groan of the landing gear and knew we were close. In moments, we'd touch down and this healing journey would be officially under way.

I can't believe I'm back, I thought as I leaned back into my seat cushion and held Adeline, now ten months old and groggy with sleep, closer to my chest. I took a deep breath, held it in for a few moments, and then released it slowly through my mouth as I started to recall the time when, at twenty-one years of age I had called this place home. It felt like a lifetime ago and yet, there I was, on a plane with all three of my children next to me, returning to a place that had completely changed my life.

It was 2005 when I joined AmeriCorps and moved from Portland, Oregon, to New York City. My assignment was with the Crown Heights Youth Collective in Crown Heights, Brooklyn, working with gang members to try and get them off the streets and into jobs and/or classrooms. Located in "the bad part of town"—the neighborhood had been the backdrop of a three-day-long race riot in 1991 that was spurred by the death of a child, and it still hadn't fully recovered, but I felt drawn toward working with disadvantaged youth and knew that, with hard work and dedication, I could make a real difference here.

I was excited for the opportunity and all that was ahead in New York City, but the thought of leaving my friends and the familiarity of home was upsetting, so when somebody mentioned Brandie Bailey, "the one with the lip piercing and beautiful smile," had recently moved to NYC, I breathed a sigh of relief. If a girl my own age who I knew from going to small punk shows around the Pacific Northwest had moved to the big city and was making it work, this meant I could too. I didn't know her well, but I remembered meeting her at a Figure Four show in Seattle years prior, and being from the same small music community we'd grown up in, I knew it meant I already had a friend there who could help me get settled. I reached out immediately to let her know I'd be moving soon.

"Ahhh so cool! You're going to love it here; I can't wait to show you around!" she messaged me back quickly. "Let's get together soon so I can introduce you to my friends, they're amazing and they'll love you!" It was 2005 and Brandie had already been living in the city for a few years, but we came from a small circle back home, and if she was willing to introduce me to potential new friends, I was going to jump on her offer.

Short on time, and without really understanding the different neighborhood structures, I found an apartment and roommate on Craigslist in the Bensonhurst neighborhood of Brooklyn. "Oh, you're out *there*..." Brandie responded when I shared with her where I'd be living. On a map it didn't look very far away from her own apartment in Williamsburg, until you pulled up the subway map and saw how many trains it would take to get from my apartment to hers. "Well, yikes," I responded, slowly realizing this was a whole new way of life I'd have to figure out. Bensonhurst wasn't terrible. It was a family neighborhood, situated on the F train, about halfway between

Coney Island and Union Square, but it did take a long time to get anywhere—especially to Brandie's apartment in Williamsburg. She and her three roommates were the only friends I'd made in the city, so I'd often take the train there on weekends and stay over until midweek when I needed to get home to do laundry or check my mail. Brandie, Mo, Colette, Jessica, and I hit it off quickly and we spent the following months together laughing and dreaming about the future. We'd stay up late watching the heaps of bootleg DVDs mailed to us every month by Mo's dad and play board games around the kitchen table while feasting on Colette's famous vegan macaroni and cheese. We'd host friends and bands visiting from around the United States, letting them play concerts on the rooftop before taking them to dinner at any of our favorite restaurants. On the cusp of gentrification sweeping through the historic Brooklyn neighborhoods, Williamsburg at the time was an odd mixture of older Hasidic Jewish residents and young hipsters covered in tattoos, with trendy new coffee shops nestled amongst age-old bodegas. You had to walk past barbed-wire enclosed repair shops to get to the new health food inspired corner store. It was a neighborhood fighting the battle of new versus old, but it was New York City in 2005, during the prime of my life, and it was everything I had dreamed it would be.

Brandie and her roommates all worked at Red Bamboo, a popular vegetarian restaurant in the city and a hot spot for young people who would chain up their fixed-gear bikes along the faded black railings. Brandie's own bike was commonly among those chained up, typically working the closing shift at the restaurant before riding home through lower Manhattan, across the Williamsburg bridge. The evening of May 8, 2005, was no different as she said goodbye and goodnight to her coworkers at Red Bamboo, hopped on her bike and began her ride home.

I hadn't officially moved into apartment 407 yet but had spent the day with the girls and decided to sleep over so I'd be close to work in Crown Heights the next morning. I was sleeping in the loft above Brandie's room, so I wrote a note for her that read, "I have to be up early tomorrow so I'm sleeping here tonight. Hope that's OK! Let's hang out tomorrow!" I slipped it under her bedroom door and quickly fell asleep.

At some point during the night, I was startled awake by the sound of my phone ringing next to me.

"Hello?" I said in a groggy voice as I answered the phone and peeked at the time on the clock, which read 4:00 a.m. *Odd.*

"Ashley!" a male voice I quickly recognized as Colette's boyfriend called out from the receiver.

"Nelson?" I asked, completely out of it.

"Ashley, wake up!" he didn't sound like himself. "I need you to listen to me!"

Something wasn't right.

"Brandie got hit."

What?

"Brandie got hit and she didn't make it."

"What?"

"She didn't make it, Ashley."

"What are you talking about?" I asked, my voice a higher tone as if accusing him of something. I sat up in bed and tried to make sense of what he was saying. "What are you talking about?" I didn't know Nelson all that well, outside of him being

Colette's boyfriend, but the tone in his voice told me something big had happened.

"Ashley, I need you to wake up." He repeated. I was up, I was awake. I just couldn't understand what he was talking about.

"I'm at the apartment—" I began explaining, but Nelson cut me off.

"Ashley, Brandie was riding her bike home last night and she was hit. She died, Ashley. She didn't make it, she died. I'm with the medical examiner now. Ashley, Brandie died."

The blood drained from my face. I didn't believe him. I dropped the phone, rushed downstairs, opened her bedroom door and...I saw my note, still on the floor. It was true. Brandie hadn't been home, she wasn't there.

My knees gave out and I fell to the hardwood floor, screaming at the top of my lungs. Marina—whose room was adjacent to the loft I'd been sleeping in only moments prior—heard me and opened her door.

"Ashley, what's wrong?" she asked, groggy with sleep.

"Brandie died!" I screamed so hard my throat burned. "She was riding her bike and got hit and SHE DIED." I said all at once, overwhelmed and consumed in tears. She was our age, beautiful and happy, with a smile that could light up an entire room. How could this be real? There's no way.

Marina was quiet for a few moments before I heard her catch her breath. She steadied herself and began walking down the stairs toward me, her body shaking as she joined me on the hardwood floor. We hugged and cried and sank into each other, not wanting to believe this could be true. We were all in our early twenties, living our best lives in the greatest city on Earth, and in a single moment, it had all come crashing down.

Colette's boyfriend, Nelson, walked in the door later that morning and gave us the only information he had. "She was riding home and stopped for a light at the intersection of Avenue A and Houston, when a garbage truck hit her and dragged her underneath its wheels..." His voice sunk low into his chest. He couldn't get his words out, and we didn't want to hear it. *How was this possible?* Brandie had been here the day before, her laughter had filled the hallways, she'd cut my hair and told me about her crush while sitting in this kitchen chair, she'd just figured out how to change her phone ringtone and picked her favorite song, "Maps." These were moments we'd just experienced as friends, as an apartment, as a household...she was only twenty-one years old, and she was just here. How was this possible she was dead? We were inconsolable. The walls of apartment 407 had never felt so small and consuming as they did that day and those following her death.

In the months following, Mo, Colette, Jessica, Nelson, and I did everything we could think of to honor Brandie and her memory. The Ghost Bike Project—a movement to bring awareness to cyclists killed—painted and donated a white ghost bike and plaque in Brandie's name and placed it at the intersection of Houston and Avenue A in lower Manhattan. We'd visit her ghost bike nearly every day, bringing flowers and notes, candles and photos, still not wanting this to be real, but grateful for the memorial and to have a place for everyone who knew and loved her to mourn and reminisce. We'd sit there for a few minutes, or a few hours, depending on the day—and often people would stop to ask what had happened, what we were doing, who it was, and why the bike was white.

"Did you know her?" Mo was asked one day while perched in front of the ghost bike.

With her bright orange hair and tiny five-foot-one frame, she looked up and nodded her head, "yes."

"She was my best friend," Mo responded.

"I was here with her the night it happened," this woman said, staring at the bike, tears apparent in her eyes, her voice shaking. "I'm so unbelievably sorry, sweetheart. I was here the night of the accident and saw it all happen. I've walked past this corner so many times since, hoping to find somebody who knew her so I could tell you...I held her hand and told her that her family loved her." With a shaky voice she continued, "I'm so, so sorry. It all happened so fast, but I want you to know I held her hand as she slipped away." The woman crouched down on the filthy New York City sidewalk next to Mo and talked through the events of that evening. Questions we had pondered, worries we'd had, thoughts too painful to bring up with one another, this woman—a perfect stranger in a city full of people—had shared our friend's final moments with her and was now sharing those moments with Brandie's best friend.

Mo came home and shared this story with all of us as we sat and listened in disbelief. The hardest part of losing Brandie, besides her actual death, had been thinking that in her final moments, she was alone, or in pain. This woman, with only a few of her words, gave us the gift of knowing she wasn't alone, and this was an interaction each of us would take with us for the rest of our lives.

There is no preparing yourself to cope with the loss of somebody close to you, but at twenty-one years old, each with our entire life ahead of us, Brandie's death shook us to the core. The type of trauma that sticks with you and leaves scars that others can't see, but you feel in the depths of your soul. The kind of trauma that affects how you live life, and makes you appreciate the friendships and relationships around you. Brandie Bailey died that spring, but her spirit and legacy lives on through Mo, Colette, Marina, me, and everybody who was lucky enough to call her a friend.

I knew that if this trip across Europe with my three children was going to be a healing journey, to honor Brian and the life he lived and legacy he left behind, it had to start in—

"Welcome to New York City!"

I opened my eyes suddenly. I had been so caught up in reminiscing these memories of my youth, I hadn't even noticed we had touched down. Addy was still sleeping, although she started squirming a bit. *Her ears are probably bothering her*, I thought as I held her tight. Kayla and I looked at each other and smiled, relieved and excited that we had finally arrived at our very first destination. This was going to be an incredible journey and it was all just beginning.

We spent the next few days walking the familiar streets of the place I'd once called home, perusing souvenirs in Times Square, riding the Staten Island Ferry for its free views of the Statue of Liberty, walking through the toy aisles of FAO Schwartz, and visiting with old friends and family who lived in the area. Our days were full of adventure and exploration—and a lot of walking. Adeline hitched a free ride in her baby carrier strapped to my chest, but Izzy and Hudson put in mile upon mile, walking the streets I'd once walked as a twenty-one-year-old, without a complaint. They were fascinated with the cars, trains, busses, and endless candy shops surrounding us, and this was further confirmation they'd do just fine in the months to come as we traveled the globe.

Our days in New York City were limited, but I was excited when my phone alerted me to a text message from John, a dear friend of mine from Hawaii who recently moved to Maryland and was now only a train ride away from where the kids and I were spending the week. "I'd love to come up for a few days if you think you'd have time!" the message read. With an eerily similar calm and kind demeanor as Brian, John was one of Brian's dive buddies and had been on the boat with Brian the day he died. He'd also helped pull my husband's body from the warm Hawaiian waters he'd drowned in and had wiped bloody foam from him mouth as he attempted CPR on the emergency boat ride back to the dock. John had witnessed my husband's death and stood next to me as I received the news that he didn't make it. John carried deep scars with him from what he experienced that day, and certainly needed a few days of laughter and fun with the us as much as we needed it with him. This would be a healing weekend for all of us and I was grateful he was willing to make the trip up.

"Plus, I've never been to New York City, so it'll be great!" he said, as I sketched out a few ideas of things to show him around town, making sure to leave time in our schedule to have dinner at Red Bamboo and visit the intersection of Houston and Avenue A.

John, Kayla, Isabel, Hudson, Adeline, and I spent the next few days taking the subway from New Jersey to Manhattan, gorging ourselves on street vendor falafel sandwiches, watching the chess players in Washington Square Park, and buying trinkets with *NYC* stamped across them. We walked past the performers in Battery Park, stopped to take photos of the brass bull in the financial district and finally found our way to the 9/11 memorial at Ground Zero where we slowly ran our fingers across the black marble plaques inscribed with the names of the thousands of victims who lost their lives on that tragic day in 2001.

"Are you tired, Hudson?" John asked my little boy, who confidently shook his head no and kept his pace next to Izzy, feeling energized knowing we were headed for a visit to FAO Schwartz, the iconic three-level toy store in midtown Manhattan, where he would get to pick out a toy of his choosing—a strategic ploy to keep this three-year-old boy walking for days.

Our days in New York City went by quickly and soon it was time for John to head home to his family in Maryland and Kasey to join us so we could begin the next leg of our journey. Our last day in Manhattan, with the kids strolling next to me, I couldn't help but think of experiencing profound loss, as I had at the age of twenty-one with losing Brandie, and then again at the age of thirty-four with losing Brian. Both of these losses had changed me on a deep, cellular level. Brandie's loss changed me into the person Brian fell in love with, and Brian's loss changed me into the woman who was about to take all three of my children on this two-month long healing journey. Navigating my way through these streets with Adeline strapped to my chest and Hudson and Izzy holding hands next to me, I understood many years ago I had initially come to New York City hoping to make change, but instead New York City had changed *me*. I walked confidently with my children—Brian's children—next to me, proud of the fact I understood that tomorrow was never guaranteed, and that we truly have to grasp any opportunity to be happy, to make more of life, to love more deeply, to live more freely. And that was exactly what my children and I were on a mission to do, one European country at a time.

Chapter Eleven

"Ewww, cheesecake!" Isabel looked at me with her nose turned up in the air, her four-almost-five-year-old expression conveying in no uncertain terms that she'd rather have the brownie in the case than the cheesecake I'd just ordered. I adjusted the baby carrier strapped to my chest with twenty-pound Adeline sound asleep inside as I rifled through my purse for my wallet.

"Tomorrow is Dadda's birthday, kiddo." I paused to look at her and smile. I could tell she was thinking through what I was saying to her. "We'll be on the airplane so I thought we could sing *Happy Birthday* to him and eat cheesecake on the plane while we fly to Amsterdam! Does that sound fun?" Her eyes became big, and a quiet smile formed on her face, a silent acknowledgment of this special day.

"But Dadda passed away, mom." Izzy grabbed my hand and looked back at the pastry case.

"I know, sweetheart, but we can still celebrate these special days for him. If he were here with us, he'd want to eat *all* the cheesecake in the whole wide world! Well, he might give you one bite," I teased her, trying to keep the conversation light, but wanting to let her know that just because Brian wasn't physically with us, he'd be a part of our family forever, and we'd make sure to celebrate the special days always.

"Mommm..." Izzy rolled her eyes and left my side in search of something more interesting than the cheesecake transaction taking place.

My little brother, Benny, chauffeured us from his home in New Jersey—where we'd spent the past few days—into New York City, before dropping us off at the JFK international airport terminal to say goodbye. *This was it.* Kasey flew in from Portland earlier in the day and now we just needed to meet up with her before embarking on this journey.

We had seven hours before our overnight flight to Amsterdam, so Kasey met us near the baggage claim, and we decided to take advantage of the USO military services offered to us as a Gold Star (military widow) family. The six of us, with all of our luggage, stroller, and gear in tow were quite the scene walking through the airport. Our first hour as a group, we worked together to figure out who would push the luggage cart, who would hold the kids' hands, carry bags, push the stroller, offer snacks, and pick things up as the kids dropped them. It was a steep learning curve and one we knew we'd have to work out in the days, weeks, and months ahead, but we were there, and we were doing it. We knew if everyone stayed safe, healthy, and with their passports, the rest would get figured out along the way.

"You're all traveling together?" The volunteer at the USO desk asked as I handed her my military ID to sign in.

"Yes, all of us. Is that OK for everyone to come in?" I asked, hesitantly. I'd been in a USO only one other time when Brian and I took the kids to Portugal and our flight out of Boston was delayed. I knew it was typically a quiet space for uniformed service members to relax before flights, but that it was open to military families as well, and there we were, all six of us and two months' worth of traveling gear in tow.

"Is your sponsor with you?" She asked, looking from me to my ID, obviously not seeing the section in the upper right corner that said sponsor-status: deceased.

"We are a Gold Star family," I said, lowering my voice. "My husband passed away in May of last year while on active duty, so it's just us."

"Oh sweetheart, I'm so sorry..." Her voice trailed off as she looked from me to the kids, to our stuff and back to me. "Please come in. Let me see if I have anything special for your children to play with." She began searching for toys and trinkets behind her desk as Kasey lined our luggage and car seats up against the wall and Kayla took the kids to the back room to get cozy for the next few hours. I stayed back to sign us in at the front desk and to chat with the volunteer as she pulled out some crayons and scratch paper for the kids.

"Where are you traveling?" She asked gently.

"Well, kind of all over," I replied, not really sure how into detail I should get with this complete stranger, before deciding *why not*? This trip was supposed to be a healing journey, and part of that healing would come from talking about Brian and the reason for this trip. So, off I went explaining.

"Two months?! All of you!? Bless your heart." Her eyes were wide as she registered what I was telling her.

"Two months. Seven countries. All of us." I smiled as I said the words out loud.

"Hey Ash, do you have Addy's bottle?" Kayla interrupted. It was getting late and Adeline wasn't sure what time zone we were in or what time it was, but she was ready for a bottle and bed.

Our flight wasn't until 11:30 p.m., so we settled into the USO and spent the next few hours enjoying the lounge area, eating snacks, playing games, and relaxing before we made our way upstairs to check in. Once there, we were confronted with pure chaos and it took us nearly two full hours to make our way through the baggage check-in. We watched the time tick by, the numbers on the clock moving faster than we were in line, the kids tired and restless, the adults nervous we wouldn't make our flight. We'd have to make a sprint to get through security and to our gate, with three kids and a stroller in tow.

"Where is your destination?" the gate agent asked.

"Amsterdam," I announced loudly, as I handed all six passports over to her, watching the clock strike 10:45 p.m. We had forty-five minutes to get three adults, three kids, a stroller, and a package of very special slice of cheesecake from the baggage drop through security, to our gate, and on the plane. We could do it. I grabbed the luggage tags from the gate agent while Kasey scooped up Hudson in her arms. Isabel jumped on Kayla's back, and I strapped Addy into her stroller. We ran and ran, hustling past luggage carts, groups of travelers—young and old, and families with kids, searching for signs that read *Security Check Point*. And then we saw the line. This line was just as long, if not longer than the one we'd just stood in to check in our bags. There was no way we'd make it. With a child attached to each of us, we approached the "special services" line and explained our flight left in thirty-five minutes. We must have looked overwhelmed, or out of our minds, but the TSA agent took pity on us and let us through this line. Fifteen minutes later we were through security, stopping only to use the bathroom to change Addy's diaper before arriving at the gate where they were already boarding. *Whew.* Somehow, we made it, and now we were off. We settled into our seats, Addy was already sound asleep—Izzy and Hudson sat next to the girls, and the six of us were ready for takeoff. Kasey, Kayla, and I looked at each other and smiled. *Time to go.*

Goodbye, America. We'll see you in a few months.

We hadn't even made it through the airplane overhead briefing before we were all sound asleep. Six hours later, I woke up to Addy yawning and rubbing her eyes, still strapped to my chest in her carrier, and looked at the flight map to see "Time to destination: forty-three minutes." I looked around to see the rest of my traveling companions still sound asleep and I smiled to myself. *These kids are such good travelers. What troopers to put up with the stuff they've been put through this past year, and now here they are, on the road for the next two months headed for strange lands without a single complaint. I'm a lucky mom.*

As the plane landed, we began gathering our stuff and I reached for the bag under my seat and saw it. *The cheesecake!*

We'd slept through the entire flight and completely forgotten about the cheesecake. We'd have to celebrate Brian's birthday when we made it to our Airbnb later that day. *Sorry babe.* We stepped off the plane and followed the crowd in front of us to customs and immigration where Kayla and Adeline collected their very first passport stamps, and then we made our way to collect our luggage, excited to finally begin this journey. An hour later, however, we were still watching the luggage conveyer belt spinning in circles, void of any actual luggage. Our luggage wasn't there. First, we were told that our luggage delay was due to a mechanical error and to keep waiting. An hour after that, a handful of weary travelers still waited and approached the lost luggage counter to finally learn there was one more container still on the plane. It took another full hour for us to retrieve our luggage and the kids' car seats. Three hours we waited for this luggage, after a full day of travel and an overnight flight. Oh, and it was Brian's birthday. We were emotional and exhausted, but we had made it to Europe and now we had our stuff. I just needed to call the shuttle I'd arranged to take us to our Airbnb. I dialed the number and gave the woman who answered the phone my reservation number.

"I'm sorry, madam, we have you booked for the shuttle service tomorrow," I was told in her thick Dutch accent.

"I'm sorry?" I asked, I must have misunderstood because of the accent.

"It looks like you're booked for the van service tomorrow, June 27," she responded.

I hadn't misunderstood. I just didn't want to hear what she was telling me.

"Umm...well, we are at the airport now. Is there any way you can change the reservation to today?" I asked, trying not to panic. Five sets of eyes cast inquisitive looks at me wondering who I was talking to and why it was taking so long to tell them we were ready for pickup.

"I'm sorry, we are completely booked for today."

"Uh-oh," I said out loud, my mind beginning to think about the Airbnb and wondering if I'd booked that for the wrong day as well. We'd taken an overnight flight and gone through a change in time zones from the West Coast to the East Coast and now to The Netherlands, and I must have miscalculated my dates when making these initial reservations. I thanked the lady on the phone and told her to cancel my shuttle for the next day and I'd figure something out. I quickly hung up the phone and looked up our Airbnb reservation.

"Well, yikes," I said out loud again. I messed up.

When I made the reservation, I must have gotten confused with all the dates—*leaving New York late at night on June 25, which is actually June 26 in Amsterdam because they are six hours ahead of New York, but nine hours ahead of home, which means that when we get there it will be a day later, so I should book the Airbnb for June 27.* There was the mistake. It was still June 26.

I couldn't believe that this was happening. I'd traveled to over twenty-five countries in my life, and I knew how time zones worked. I knew how dates changed and overnight flights worked, how had I messed this up? And with the kids? And Kasey and Kayla, all who were looking to me to take care of this stuff. I had convinced each of them to come with me on this trip,

I had a responsibility to each of them to make this a positive and safe experience. We were less than twenty-four hours into this trip and already I had slept through Brian's birthday celebration, we had dealt with a potential lost luggage situation, and now, we didn't have anywhere to stay because I accidently booked the house on the wrong day. *What did I get us all into? I want to cry. I want Brian here to help me figure this out.*

I turned around and looked at the five faces and pile of luggage looking back at me, wondering what I was doing. I knew this was all on me to take care of. I realized I had two options: I could either fall apart right there and then, or I could figure it out. As I'd decided early on during this grief journey, I was going to figure it out. For me, for the kids, for us as a family, I was going to pull myself together and make it work.

"I'll be right back, guys. I have to make a quick call." I looked at the group looking back and me and excused myself. This was a long shot, but it was worth making the call to ask.

I called our Airbnb host and explained the situation, asking if there was any chance that we could check into the house a day early.

"No problem. I'll message you the key code and hope you enjoy your stay." He said back to me. *Whew.* One hurdle down. Now to find a taxi that could fit all of us and our stuff.

"Funny story," I said, returning to my travel buddies and the pile of luggage—all waiting for a place to go. "I booked our house for the wrong day..." I said slowly. I could see their eyes widen, wondering where we would go and how I was going to fix this.

"I know. I'm sorry, but I got it sorted out and we can head there now!"

I felt the collective sigh of relief from myself, Kasey, and Kayla as we loaded our luggage onto the buggy and headed outside to find a taxi.

"Lots of children!" the driver made sure to comment. "You're all together? From America?"

"Yep!" I replied, unsure as to where he was going with this.

"Where are the husbands?" He asked in a non-accusatory tone but rather one that was filled with genuine surprise.

"Oh." I didn't know what to say. Well, actually I did. *My husband died a year ago and my children and I are on this journey to find peace and try to heal from this horrible tragedy that struck my young family.* But I didn't want to tell him. We had just met, and this was probably the last time we would ever cross paths, so I simply said, "No husbands, just us!" And I offered a small laugh, trying to settle his curiosity.

"Wow, no men?" he pushed further. "All women? This is not something we see here!"

At that point, I simply raised my head upward to acknowledge I had heard him and briefly met his eyes through the rearview mirror he was using to glance at us from time to time. "Hudson is the man of our group!" Kayla said from her place next to our lone male traveling companion. Before he pointed it out, it hadn't really crossed my mind that we looked like an odd combination, given the absence of grown men in our party. But there it was, and there we were, and if people were uncomfortable with the idea of us traveling without any grown men, then my three-year-old son, Hudson, could be our spokesperson.

Once we finally arrived at the house, we were beyond exhausted. Our bodies were still on New York time, which

meant it was time for bed, but it was early afternoon in Amsterdam, the sun was shining, and we needed to get a few groceries
to stock the fridge for our week in The Netherlands. We spent
the next hour walking to the store to grab a few essentials, and
since the day-old cheesecake had been left on the airplane, we
stopped for soft serve ice cream on the way back, using this
time to sing *Happy Birthday* to Brian. We made our way back
to the house, walking through the red brick entrance adorned
with vines from the plants growing in the yard and then carefully
explored the eclectic home-turned-Airbnb rental just outside of
the Amsterdam city limits. Izzy and Hudson deciding to share
the room with the yellow wooden Tonka truck bed we'd seen
in the online photos, and we all were excited about the fact it
was now officially early evening in Amsterdam. I gave Addy a
bottle and said goodnight. I could hear the footsteps of Kasey,
Kayla, Izzy, and Hudson upstairs, but I was too tired—emotionally, physically, and psychologically—to pay much attention. It
had been a rough twenty-four hours and I was ready for a good
night's sleep. I closed my eyes, thinking of Brian and wishing
him a happy birthday, vaguely daydreaming of how we would
have spent the day had he been there with us, before drifting off.

I hadn't been asleep long before I was startled awake by Izzy
coming into my room saying she couldn't sleep because Hudson
was moving all around in bed, so she wanted to sleep with me.
Five minutes later, Hudson—and "Baby Bear"—appeared and
crawled into bed with us too. So, there we were, 5,000 miles from
home, and both kids were asleep in my bed. "Baby Bear" was
an old, formerly brown but now grey stuffed animal that Hudson
had always been obsessed with. This smelly, raggedy bear was

his dearest possession, and he'd tell anyone who would listen, "I love Baby Bear and Baby Bear loves me." Hudson refused to leave Baby Bear at home, which naturally meant Baby Bear now had just as many stamps in his passport as Hudson did.

Adeline was asleep in the living room in the "baby box" our Airbnb host put together—apparently his own from when he was a child—which was a large wooden box with wooden slats all around the edges and a thick wooden lid I propped open (think baby prison cell, but more primitive) meant to keep her contained, but which also served to accentuate her cries of protest for me putting her in such a thing at bedtime. Kayla was now sleeping in the single yellow Tonka truck shaped bed that the kids abandoned, and Kasey was alone in the sweltering attic. We didn't have the luxuries of home, but we were together, on the adventure of a lifetime, and that would get us through the next few months of random sleeping arrangements this trip would bring us.

Adeline woke up around midnight to eat, so I gave her a bottle and put her back in the wooden box, at which time she cried out again in protest. I was exhausted and my body confused with what time it actually was, so my plan was to let her cry it out until she fell back asleep. Eight minutes later, her cries stopped, and I heard creaking steps outside my door. I looked up and there was Kasey holding a smiling Adeline.

"Addy was crying," Kasey whispered, proud of the fact she'd woken up and anxious to earn her keep on this trip by helping out with Addy so that I could get some sleep.

"I just gave her a bottle," I whispered to her. "She needs to go back to sleep now."

"Oh, I'm sorry," Kasey replied in hushed tones, "I thought maybe you didn't hear her, I was going to give her a bottle! What a stinker!" We laughed at Addy, who was wide awake now and super proud of herself for waking up not one, but two people who could now give her attention. It was going to take some effort to get her adjusted to Amsterdam time.

We woke up bright and early the next day, excited about our first full day of exploring Amsterdam. We walked the twenty minutes from our rented farmhouse to the train station, where we passed fields of tulips and wildflowers, brightly colored homes with yards filled with pigs and chickens grazing in the fields, and over cobblestone roads. We zigzagging between people commuting to and from the city on their bicycles. It was a spectacular sight, and this very first walk to the train station had the distinct feeling of being in The Netherlands.

After a chorus of "Are we there yet?" from Izzy and "This walk is taking for-e-verrrrr" from Hudson, we finally found the train station and after a bit of a debacle with our American debit cards, purchased the train tickets, found our platform, and were soon bound for the city! Hudson *loves* trains so he was ecstatic—Izzy, not so much, and Adeline was indifferent, only concerned about the snacks we'd brought along for her. Nevertheless, we made it and were promptly greeted with the realization we were underdressed. This was Europe in summer, we were expecting soaring temperatures but instead were quick to realize it was about 65 degrees and windy! We walked through Amsterdam Central past all the marijuana shops and restaurants until we found a souvenir shop that sold sweatshirts. Sixty-five Euros later, we were ready to begin our day now fully armed with warmer clothing. We strolled down the central area and stopped for lunch—cheese toasties (grilled cheese as we call them in the States)—then continued on past the canals and over the bridges until we came to a little bar with outside seating where we stopped for an afternoon gin and tonic and some people watching. At twenty years old, this was Kayla's first (legal) alcoholic drink, so we raised our glasses, the kids with their apple juice, and toasted Amsterdam, each other, and the kids.

After the ice melted and we'd finished our drinks, we started walking again, eventually ending up back near the train station by the local tour company and decided to take in the sights of the city by boat. We raced to get the outside seats and spent the next hour in the sun, floating through the canals of Amsterdam. The sights and sounds of the city were exactly what I expected of Amsterdam: everyone on bicycles with big baskets attached to the front, canals that cut through the city streets, boats and barges filled with people from all over the world. It was an experience you can't have by looking at a photo and one of the many joys of travel to see what a place looks like, to hear what it sounds like, what it smells like and feels like. Travel isn't just about what you're seeing or doing, but rather the experience of it hitting all your senses. I felt proud in this moment, looking around the city, at my kids and friends as they looked around, knowing despite the initial hurdles we'd encountered the day before, this would be an incredible, life-changing trip and I was proud of myself for making it happen.

"Has anyone seen my purse?" Kasey asked, moments after walking back in the door from our first day out in the city.

"Huh?" Kayla and I asked in unison.

"Have you seen my purse?" Kasey asked again, the sound of panic more apparent in her voice this time as she began rummaging through the bags of treasures that we'd brought home with us.

"You had it on the train, remember? You grabbed your Chapstick out of it." Kayla said as Kasey finished looking through the bags attached to Adeline's stroller, suddenly in a full-blown panic upon realizing she'd left it on the train.

Thankfully, she'd left her passport at the house, but she was now without her wallet, debit card, driver's license, three granola bars, and some Chapstick. We filed a report with the Metro and hoped for a positive outcome, but we knew the purse was long gone. The kids were safe and we had our passports, and I told everyone before we even began that as long as these two things remained true throughout our travels, everything would be ok. This would be a trip of memorable and learning experiences for everyone.

The next day we set out for the beach. It was the one thing I wanted to make sure we did in each country—to get to the coast, or at least a body of water. Today was a sunny day and we all yearned for some fresh air. I called a taxi company, telling them we had six passengers and would need a van of some sort. Thirty minutes later, we stood outside our Airbnb rental and watched as a vintage white limousine pulled down our street. *Is that our taxi?* We looked at each other, half smiling, half laughing, shrugging and waiting to see if it stopped at our house.

"Ashley?" the man asked in his thick Dutch accent as the oversized car pulled to a stop in front of us.

"Yep, that's us!" I said, trying to hold back the laughter brewing inside of me at how ridiculous this sight would be in the small coastal town of Egmond aan Zee, three adults and three young children spilling out of this 1980s style limo for a day at the beach.

"You're traveling here from America? The children are so young." Our driver started in with the conversation as he guided our "taxi" through the winding roads hugging the coastline as we drove toward the North Sea. We spent the next forty minutes explaining—again—that it was just the six of us traveling, the kids were all mine, we would be spending the next two months traveling through Europe and no, this isn't something Americans typically do either.

"We're here!" I exclaimed as our driver expertly maneuvered his large car into three parking spots in front of a wall of bicycles, glimmers of the blue ocean off just in the distance below us. We all piled out, paying him, thanking him, and making arrangement for a pickup time and place in just a few hours.

"Can we get some coffee really quick?" Kasey asked, as we walked past a small café with people sitting outside and signs advertising soft serve ice cream and Dutch pastries.

"Do you have iced coffee?" Kasey asked the waiter.

"Cafe?" the man replied, wanting to make sure he'd understood Kasey's request.

"Iced coffee," Kasey repeated, making a gesture of holding a coffee cup, not realizing to everyone around her, she had a thick American accent.

"Ahh, koffie?" he asked, now understanding what she was looking for.

"Yes please, with ice?" she asked, a little slower this time.

"Soft ice?" the waiter repeated back to her, an unsure look on his face.

"Yes, please. Coffee with ice," Kasey repeated.

"Soft ice? For the koffie?" this waiter was becoming more and more unsure as the seconds ticked by.

"Yes, please," Kasey said in a brave tone, feeling confident they were both on the same page.

The waiter walked back to the kitchen, a slightly confused look on his face, where we watched as he spoke to two of his coworkers, who all looked at us, and back at each other, shrugging and obviously talking about the conversation that had just transpired at our table. *Maybe they don't get a lot of American tourists in here, especially groups like us. Were they wondering where our husbands were too? Is iced coffee not a thing here in The Netherlands?*

Moments later, our waiter appeared again, charging toward our small table, holding a small cup of espresso in one hand and a cup of vanilla soft serve ice cream in the other. Kasey, Kayla, and I looked at each other before doubling over in laughter while Izzy and Hudson were both excited to see ice cream suddenly appear at the table.

"Soft ice," the waiter said, looking from Kasey and back to the tray containing the contents he'd just brought to her. His facial expression reading, *this must be an American thing.*

Kasey smiled back at him, picked up a spoonful of vanilla ice cream, and stirred it into her tiny espresso cup, shrugging and saying, "Oh well, it's like cream and sugar in one!"

We were floored! We couldn't stop laughing about it as we made our way down the beach. The weather was spectacular and, as it was a Saturday, the beach was crowded. Obviously, the first thing all of us wanted to do was get our feet wet, but as soon as we approached the water, we noticed what could only be described as thousands of tiny purple jellyfish! People around us were scooping them out of the water, placing them in piles on the beach, catching them in nets and looking as shocked as we were at the sight of so many in one place. With the kids especially saddened that the presence of these meant we couldn't go swimming, we decided to cut short our time on shore, take some photos and head back home to rest.

"I need just a minute," I told Kasey and Kayla as they started walking away from the beach with the kids. I walked closer to the edge of the water and found a broken seashell discarded in the sand. I had brought some of Brian's ashes with me for this journey and had plans of spreading him throughout our trip in as many bodies of water as we were able to visit. If he couldn't be with us on our journey, I'd leave a part of him in each of our destinations, knowing there was no other place he'd rather be than with us, his family, and on, near, or in the ocean. I held the shell in my hand and slowly poured some of Brian's ashes into it. I took a deep breath and gently blew this little bit of him into the water. *If you fall asleep down by the water,* I hummed to myself and watched as the waves carried him out to sea.

We spent the next few days in The Netherlands making incredible memories. We visited the iconic windmills, ate delicate, buttery, chocolate-dipped *stroopwafel* from the local farmers market, tried on wooden clogs, and even ventured down the streets of the red light district for some ultra-touristy sightseeing. Time flew by at the speed of light, and before we knew it, our time in Amsterdam came to an end. There was however, one more stop I wanted to make before leaving The Netherlands: the Anne Frank House. I had talked to Izzy about Anne Frank and what she had been through before we even began our journey, so she had heard the name before, and knew we'd be visiting a place of incredible historic significance, where a girl only a little older than Izzy experienced something terrible. She had quickly shown interest in this brave girl's story and Izzy's curiosity and willingness to learn more was evident through the many questions she asked me about her. I knew that visiting the house-turned-museum would be as important to me as it was to her, and it showed from the moment we walked into it.

"Mama," Isabel whispered as she tugged at my shirt. "This is the bookcase that Anne Frank hid behind!" Her big blue eyes were filled with wonder and respect for what the Jewish sixteen-year-old had had to endure in her brief life while hiding from the Nazis.

With Adeline strapped to my chest in her baby carrier, I listened intently to the audiotape we had been given at the entrance of the museum and even though I tried not to miss anything, I couldn't help but notice just how attentive Izzy was listening to her audiotape. At only four years of age, Izzy could sense this was an important story and was quick to point things out to us as we walked up and down the stairs, looking at photos and memorabilia from Anne Frank's time spent hiding within these walls.

Once we were done with our tour, we walked through the bookstore gift shop where I bought Izzy and Adeline each a red diary that looked just like the one Anne Frank had confided her thoughts to during her years in hiding. Izzy brought the red cloth book close to her chest, squeezed it as if it were her most prized possession and proceeded to ask for a pen to write her name in it right away, "Just like Anne Frank did!" she squealed.

"She's so stinking smart," Kayla said to me once we were back home, watching Izzy lay down on the floor to craft her very first diary entry in her new red journal. "She was so engrossed in that museum and who Anne Frank was. She even knew her dad's name was Otto and that they all went to the Nazi prison. What four-year-old understands all of that?" Kayla was as impressed as I was.

"Truthfully, I don't think adults give kids enough credit. They are so smart and capable of understanding things, if we take the time to teach it to them. I don't want my kids to just read about things like this in their school history books, I want them to know what they look like in real life and to be able to make their own memories of things like this." I lowered my voice so that Izzy wouldn't pick up on our conversation and continued, "I'm sure I'll get criticized by people for taking my kids to places like these, and explaining things such as Holocaust to them, but I explain these concepts in a way they'll understand, and I know that education is the best gift I can give them, so I'm going to." I said, understanding the way I'm choosing to raise my three young children is unconventional, but also understanding the importance of experience, and proud of myself for providing that to them. "I know she won't be able to remember everything about our time at the Anne Frank House, but I know that once she's older and reads about Anne Frank in her history books, I will have the chance to remind her, through photos and stories, that she went there to visit the actual house and we created memories here." Kayla smiled at me and put her arm around my shoulder, thankful for the opportunity to experience these moments with us, as we sat on the couch together, watching Izzy scribble away in her brand new diary.

Chapter Twelve

"**M**ama, I have to go *pottyyyy,*" I heard Hudson's little voice wail from the back seat of our taxi. We concluded our time in The Netherlands, and were now on our way to Norway. Kasey and Hudson spent some one-on-one time together in The Netherlands, and after a few pep-talks and positive reinforcement, three-year-old Hudson was leaving The Netherlands a completely potty-trained little man! It was an accomplishment worth celebrating, but also one of worry as we were only twenty minutes into our forty-five-minute drive to the airport!

"Can you hold it buddy? We're almost there," I lied, cringing at the knowledge we'd have at least another twenty minutes until we could get him to a bathroom.

"Yes, mama!" he sang from his car seat, proud of the fact he was officially potty-trained, and was therefore now a big boy.

Twenty-five minutes later, we pulled into the airport drop-off lane where we grabbed our luggage and zipped through the crowds of people in search of a bathroom, making it just in time. The six of us celebrated Hudson and this milestone, also laughing with each other that we—and now all of you—will always remember the time and place where Hudson was potty-trained. I'm sure he'll be unhappy with me later in life when he reads this, but great job, bud! So proud of you.

Oslo, Norway. Wow. Prior to this moment, if you asked me what I considered to be the most beautiful place on the planet, I would have told you it was a two-way tie between the Oregon coast and Ireland. Both full of hidden gems, with miles of frigid-cold coastlines and trees a shade of green only found in nature.

Brian had been to Norway a few times on work trips with the navy, and every time he returned home, he'd tell me, "You'll love it there, Ash! I can't wait to show you. It's like the Oregon coast, but better!" His photos proved that Norway was indeed beautiful, but there was no way it could compare to the most beautiful place on Earth—in my opinion—until, I arrived in Norway and witnessed it with my own eyes. From the moment we piled into our rented car and left the airport, we drove amongst the towering trees hugging the two-lane road, and glimpsed the North Sea straight ahead with reflections of white sailboat hulls bouncing off the deep blue-green water of the ocean. I felt "it." *This is what Brian was talking about.* I had been in the country for thirty minutes, but already I felt I was part of it. *I could live here.* I looked in the rear-view mirror as five sets of eyes looked back at me and said, "You guys, I love it here!"

We spent the next hour driving through mazes of tunnels and getting turned around a few different times, but I didn't care.

We'd emerge from a tunnel, pull the car over, wait for the GPS to recalibrate, and then head in the opposite direction we'd just been traveling. The ocean to our left, the trees to our right, my three children in the backseat excited about the adventures ahead in a place their dadda had told them about. I felt a magnetic force pulling me to this place; I'd never been there before, but in a strange way it felt like home. Brian had left a piece of his heart in Norway, and now we were here to experience it for ourselves. These were the moments I was desperate for and was grateful to have, and I'm sure of it, I was now taking in sights of the most beautiful place on Earth.

An hour later we pulled down the gravel driveway of our Airbnb rental in Asker, Norway. What lay before us was a bright red farmhouse set back amidst a grove of colossal trees with a trampoline in the front yard and a wooden deck on either side of the house. It was stunning. We piled out of the car and walked around the house to the back deck where we were met with a view that left us all speechless. We stood with our mouths gaped open—and our eyes squinting shut—as we stood in awe of the mighty North Sea just below us. The ocean, the trees, the sunshine, the fresh air, this place had it all.

"This view is like a fairy tale!" Kayla chimed in. This was such an understatement, but there really were no words to describe the immense beauty surrounding us.

"Mama! Can we go on the trampoline!?" Izzy asked excitedly from her place on the deck. She had taken fifteen seconds to experience the beauty Norway had to offer and she was now ready to proceed with being a kid—a kid with access to a trampoline in the front yard of our rental house.

"Sure, kiddo." I smiled. This was a healing journey for all of us and part of that healing meant taking advantage of the opportunities and moments that would bring joy. *There isn't much that can bring joy to a four-year-old faster than bouncing on a trampoline with her mom.*

"I'll race you!" I shouted before taking off in a sprint, leaving the deck and stunning views right where they were for the time being. They'd been there for millions of years and would continue to do so. This moment with my baby girl would come and go in a flash.

A short while later, after taking turns bouncing each other on the trampoline and Kayla attempting—and failing—to teach Kasey how to do a backflip, we had claimed rooms in the house, popped in to the local market for some groceries, and were ready to settle in for the night. The evening air was brisk, but we didn't want to miss out on a single moment of being in Norway, so we grilled veggie burgers on the outside deck and listened to music while the kids played in the yard and the rain moved in. We found comfort under the porch, and Izzy and Hudson curled up in blankets next to Kayla and me, while we all laughed at Kasey who sat in a wicker chair half under the deck, half in the rain, clearly unbothered by the fact that half of her body was getting soaked. Adeline had already gone to sleep for the night, and I looked at Hudson and Isabel as they laughed uncontrollably at Kasey. Her new, gray Amsterdam sweatshirt was now completely wet, but she would do anything to make my children smile. I sat back in my wicker chair and watched the entire scene unfold, unable to keep myself from smiling and laughing at the sound of my kids happy. Moments such as these were the ones we sought on this trip. The moments where the scent of fresh air and sound of your kids laughter made you feel at peace. The moments where you realized in a single instant how valuable these small droplets of time really are, and how grateful and proud you are that this is your story, and that of your kids. The moments where you realize the experiences are what's important and to make them count. These are the good ones.

I had planned the basics for us in each of the countries we'd be visiting; transportation, accommodations, and a basic itinerary, but I didn't schedule any activities. I had, of course, at least one specific landmark I wanted to see in each place, but I didn't necessarily want to micro-plan our vacation, in case something surprising and unexpected came up along the way. I wanted to have the flexibility to change plans. Traveling with small kids and trying to plan around their mealtimes, nap times, and so on put us at the mercy of their schedules and we needed to take each day as it came and make plans from there.

Our second day in Norway we decided to drive into Oslo and find a hop-on, hop-off bus tour so we could catch the basic layout of the city and see where we might want to spend more time in the days following. We squeezed our oversized—by European standards—car into a spot in front of the Viking Ship museum and caught the first bus we saw which took us downtown to the Oslo City Hall, where the Nobel Peace Prize was awarded. Knowing this was something you could literally only see in this one place on Earth, we toured the building, walked through the gift shop and bought little trinkets—such as bracelets made by women who had experienced and survived human trafficking, bookmarks created by political prisoners and various other items—keeping in mind they'd have to fit in our back-packs for seven more weeks. By the time we finished there and explored the boardwalk along the pier, the kids were hungry and ready to relax for a bit.

Twenty minutes later, the kids were *cheers*-ing their grilled cheese sandwiches while we toasted our gin and tonics in celebration of the beautiful day we were spending together in Norway.

"What should we do next?" I asked the group, my stomach now full of piping hot French fries and a cold drink.

"I want to go on a boat, mama!" Hudson exclaimed next to me, ketchup dripping down his left cheek, his eyes glued to the array of blue and white fishing vessels docked at the marina in front of us.

"Yeah? You got it, bud. Let's do it!" I smiled back at him. There was no need to think about it. I picked up my phone and fifteen minutes later had six tickets booked for the afternoon boat tour of Oslo. We had a bit of time, so we finished our lunch and drinks and began walking down the pier to meet our boat. The sun was shining, the sea was shimmering, and this place was my idea of paradise. With my kids and friends in tow, I looked down at my phone to see the blue GPS dot began to blink, indicating we were close to our destination, and as I looked back up, the flash of something caught my eye. I blinked my eyes closed, prepared to see the reflection of our tour boat in the bright sunlight, but as I opened my eyes, I saw it again and stopped in my tracks. Hudson, who had been holding my hand, halted next to me, the flash catching his attention too.

"Mama! It's Dadda!!" He squealed and took off running, releasing my hand in the process.

I froze.

In front of me was a life-size silver statue of a scuba diver standing on the edge of the pier. The sunshine reflecting off its shiny surface, onto the water, and back onto our faces as Hudson ran toward it. I watched as my three-year-old ran with his arms outstretched, my brain trying to catch up with my eyes, and even more so with my heart as I took in the words Hudson just uttered and the sight in front of me. Hudson took his final steps toward the silver statue and I watched, still frozen in place, as he wrapped his little arms around the statue's leg.

Oh no.

I felt the emotion of the moment in the pit of my stomach before I felt the hot tears in my eyes. I smiled as the tears cascaded down my cheeks, unsure if this was a happy moment or a sad one.

"Hudson, that's not really Dadda," Izzy chimed in, her voice breaking the moment as she took the opportunity to grab hold of my now-vacant hand that Hudson's had occupied only moments prior. I used my free hand to switch my phone into camera mode and captured the image of Hudson hugging the leg of the silver scuba diver statue, now both looking out at the sea in front of them.

Kayla and Kasey stared at me, the emotion of the moment apparent on their faces, unsure of what to say but sensing that this moment was special. No words were necessary. The silence that surrounded us as we looked at Hudson hugging the scuba diver statue spoke to each of us. It reminded us why we were there. Why we had embarked on this trip. Why we needed to be on this trip. The scuba diver statue was a symbol of Oslo, one that reassured people of the sea that they could rest easy, because the scuba diver had the watch.

Let's go dive Norway, babe! It will be one of those places we'll remember forever. He'd been right. I wasn't diving, but this was a place and a moment I knew I'd remember forever.

As our scheduled departure grew closer, we left the statue and arrived at the pier where a sailor welcomed us aboard. During the boat tour, I scattered Brian's ashes in the Norwegian waters. Even though I was sad and upset, I also found a sense of comfort and solace in knowing that Brian would have been so happy to be returned to a place he loved so much. It's as if the silver scuba diver statue had been a sign from the universe that this was the right place to set him free. *You've got the watch now, sweetheart.*

The next morning, we took turns trying to figure out how to work the coffee maker that had come with the house—Europe's version of a single serving brewer—complete with an instruction book printed entirely in Norwegian. Kasey eventually figured it out and we spent the next few hours drinking hot coffee on the porch while the kids jumped on the trampoline and Adeline played with some blocks. Eventually we all piled back into the car for the twenty-minute drive into the town of Asker. We parked along a busy street and walked through the different shops, eyeing things we wanted to buy but we knew wouldn't fit into our backpacks, before coming across a coffee shop with outdoor seating. We each ordered an iced coffee—coffee with actual ice this time—and after two nights of veggie burgers at the house, felt ready to try a traditional Norwegian delicacy in the form of an egg custard tart. We *oooh*'d and *ahhh*'d about how yummy it was. The crust was buttery and flaky and dissolved into thousands of tiny pastry crumbs that got all over our faces and clothes with each bite. The egg custard was thick and smooth…firmer than a *crème brûlée* and sweet with a touch of vanilla. Addy went back for second and third portions before we had consumed all of it, and it was time to move on. We found a park nearby and let Izzy and Hudson run around and find kids their own age to play with, despite the fact they didn't speak the same language.

"What time is it, anyway?" I asked the girls once we were back home. The kids were finally tucked into bed, and fell asleep lightning fast from the day's adventures. Kasey, Kayla, and I sat in the wicker chairs on the porch, enjoying a glass of gin and the quiet of the evening. With the quiet, however, came nature's song. Insects twittered and birds sang intermittently in the growing dusk. I didn't know birds sang at night. Even though the sky was still light, I knew it was getting late—despite the trickery of the "midnight sun" during Norwegian summers. I picked up my phone and saw that it was nearly midnight.

"Aghh! It's way past my bedtime!" I said as I sipped the last of my drink, the ice cubes making a clinking sound as they hit my teeth. "I'm headed to sleep. Goodnight, guys!" I smiled and walked up the wooden staircase in search of my bed and a good night's sleep.

The next day, after our morning coffee and trampoline routine, we looked at a map and located the town of Tonsberg. On Brian's last visit to Norway, he had called to tell me that he and his coworker, Alex; a seasoned and well-traveled sailor Brian had met while stationed in Washington, had visited this town, and climbed up the steps to Castle Tower within the Tonsberg Fortress. Dating back to the 1300s, this castle offered a foreboding presence to the would-be enemies it was built to keep away, but now delivered unparalleled views of the city and country below to its many visitors each year—including Brian and Alex, and now the six of us.

"Izzy, Hudson," I called. "Come here, I want to tell you something."

With Adeline strapped to my back in her baby carrier, I did my best to squat down next to them so I could look into their eyes. I reached for their little hands and said, "I want to tell you something really special." The kids nodded, clearly annoyed that I was taking them away from their turn at pointing the now-defunct cannon toward the valley below. "Do you want to know something really cool? Last time Dadda was in Norway, he came to this castle and stood right where you guys are!"

Their eyes lit up and I could see them processing the words I was sharing with them.

"But Mama, Dadda passed away. I thought he's diving forever, how did he come here?" Izzy questioned as thoughts of her dad standing in this same spot filled her mind.

"I know, sweetheart, but he came here before he passed away. Isn't this really special that he was here, and now you're here in the same spot he was?" I asked, not sure of how she'd respond to the question but relieved when she squeezed my hand and shook her head "yes" before asking if she could go back to her turn at the cannon.

The kids and I were standing in a place where Brian once stood. These were the same sights Brian had described to me on the phone, the same views he'd taken in with his own eyes, the same memories he'd made. We were somehow retracing his steps, and I knew that he would have been so proud and happy for us to visit this castle, climb up the watch tower, and enjoy these moments as a family, even if he couldn't physically be with us. I closed my eyes briefly and talked to him in silence, thanking him for guiding me there, for gifting me the strength and courage to get to this moment, for the treasure and experience I was passing on to our children.

We spent our next few days exploring the Norwegian coastline, buying souvenirs, visiting the coffee shop for more Norwegian egg custard treats—and finally stopping for an afternoon swim in the frigid waters of the Norwegian Sea, not willing to leave Norway without at least a dip in the ocean.

"I'll do it if you will!" Kayla looked from me to the jumping platform hovering twenty feet over the ocean and then back to me.

"Don't threaten me with a good time!" I teased before kicking off the sandals that had now seen two European countries and were holding up despite the miles I'd put on them in the past few weeks.

"Really?" She laughed, now hesitating as to what she'd just agreed to.

We climbed the tower to its top and made the terrible mistake of looking down over the edge. Even though we were only three flights of stairs off the ground, the deep blue sea was seemingly a thousand feet below us, with white-peaked waves lapping at the rocks below. Kayla and I spent the next ten minutes trying to convince each other to climb back down. It wasn't until a ten-year-old blonde-haired, blue-eyed girl appeared on the ladder out of nowhere, walked right past us, and jumped into the water below, that we felt ridiculous for hesitating. Izzy and Hudson started cheering "Go Mama!" from the beach while Kasey videotaped our less-than-graceful jump off the platform, splashing into the waters below. *Brrrr.*

We had made a splash in Norway in more ways than one, accomplishing exactly what we had intended to do here. The kids and I laughed, cried, reminisced, mourned and most importantly, made incredible memories together as a family. It was sad to say goodbye to Norway, to the red farmhouse, and all that had transpired there over the past ten days, but I was looking forward to all that was ahead, including the next stop on our itinerary. The next morning, we woke up early and drove our car back through the same long and winding roads, this time the trees to our left, the ocean to our right, as we made our way back to the airport. Next stop: Poland!

Chapter Thirteen

"Oh my…" I gasped, more to myself than to my friends seated next to me, the words escaping my lips before my eyes had time to catch up with the sights in front of me. We had left the airport in search of our apartment in Warsaw and while I didn't have any real expectations of what to expect from the sights and sounds of the city; it surely wasn't *this*. The Polish bakery in my childhood neighborhood had painted a slight vision in my head of stocky men and women standing outside their pierogi shops, inviting us in for friendly banter before squishing the kids' cheeks between their hard-working hands upon entry. This, however, was not the vision or experience we were greeted with. Instead, we clung tightly to our seatbelts as our driver maneuvered through pothole-filled streets, turning left, then right, past graffiti embellished ruins of what I assumed were once bustling centers for commerce, but whose rubble was now surrounded by barbed wire fences and a large homeless population coming and going through they holes they'd cut in it.

Warsaw—this portion of it at least—had a drab, eerie feeling to it. A vague familiarity, but also like nothing I'd seen before.

"What happened to these buildings?" I asked our driver out of curiosity. They looked like they'd once belonged there, but now stood vacant, their design and presence reminding me so much of Moscow, Russia, and the buildings I'd walked past in its city center years prior.

"These are from when we were under communist control." He explained in clear, almost unaccented English. "Our government is still trying to rebuild but undergoing a lot of change." I have always loved history—specifically military and war history—but there were only a few cities around the world I'd been to where you could physically see the direct effects and devastation brought about by them. Warsaw, Poland, was one of them.

I turned to look at Kasey and Kayla who were also staring out their windows. They looked shell-shocked. Kayla clenched her teeth, quite obviously uncomfortable, as she'd never seen a city like this before. It was worlds away from the idyllic, *Sound-of-Music*-like surroundings of Norway.

"You guys, we're in Poland!" I offered with the most enthusiasm I could muster. Regardless of our initial impressions on the drive through town, we were there to experience what the country had to offer and as long as we all kept a good attitude, this would be a positive experience for us. We had one week in this country, a place none of us had ever been, a place we'd all been looking forward to visiting.

The main reason I'd included Poland on our travel itinerary was to visit the Auschwitz concentration camp. Auschwitz. *Even typing the name sends shivers down my spine.* One single name, one so powerful that my body physically and emotionally reacts to as it conjured images of darkness, sadness, insurmountable horror, fear, pain, and death. Knowing we'd be setting foot on these death camps was a humbling experience, but one we were incredibly grateful for.

Auschwitz was a place I'd studied throughout my childhood and college years and one I knew was important to see in my lifetime. Being that we were on a No-Bucket-List trip—a healing journey to remind ourselves that tomorrow isn't guaranteed and to take advantage of these opportunities today—I felt strongly that we needed to include this stop in our travels; however, I also knew that visiting Auschwitz would affect me. Given the already delicate emotional state I was in, visiting a place of such incomprehensible suffering, sadness and sorrow could potentially send me back into a state of depression, but just like everything else put in front of me this past year, I knew that wasn't going to deter me and I was going to do it no matter what.

We hired a driver to take us the four hours from our apartment in Warsaw to Auschwitz in the town of Oświęcim (pronounced awsh-vyen-cheem). This drive was much more comfortable than our initial trip into Warsaw. We wound through country roads and past roadside stands and small, bustling villages. Our driver was a man our own age, who eventually confided he had two daughters, aged five and seven. I asked him if he'd taken them to Auschwitz yet and he replied rather sternly, "No, it's not a place for kids. Maybe when they're older." He was friendly and very kind to us, but he was the second native I'd spoken to in as many days who insisted they wouldn't bring their kids there. I contemplated his response, trying to decide if it was because he didn't think kids should be exposed to the realities of war, or if people saw kids as a nuisance in a place where others were trying to mourn. The scenery was beautiful; we drove through a small village with houses on either side of the two-lane road, front yards whose stone fences contained yards of green and yellow flowers, a red front door standing out against the stark white walls of one house, deep-blue wooden shutters on another. I reached for my camera to film a little bit of our drive and had just hit "record" as our van turned another corner. I looked up to see another small house to our right and trained my camera forward on the road ahead when I saw it... the barbed wire fence and watch towers just ahead.

Oh my....

"Is that...it?" I asked as the color drained from my face.

"It is," he replied, his voice void of the emotion I was feeling within, obviously used to this sight after five years of providing these tours. I looked back at the girls, Kasey was already in tears, Kayla with a pained look on her face, and me with my hand on my chest. I was trying to keep my heart from breaking. The sight of this first camp coming into view had us speechless. And then we drove over the train tracks—the same ones we'd seen in the pictures and movies. The ones we'd read about in history books. The train tracks that had carried fathers and husbands, wives and mothers, kids just like Izzy, Hudson, and Adeline, people just like us, into that exact spot and to their deaths. There they were. And just like that, we crossed over them, drove another mile down the road and parked the van.

I was sick to my stomach. I did my best to take a few deep breaths and speak very calmly to Izzy and Hudson in the back seat as I said, "Hey, guys, do you remember what we talked about last night? We need to be on our best behavior today. This is a place where a lot of people passed away, and a lot of people you're going to see today are going to be very sad about it. Just like we were really sad when Dadda passed away, all of these people are really sad about the people who passed away here. You might see me and Kasey and Kayla crying today too. We're OK, just a little sad. I want you to ask any questions you have as we walk through, but you need to be very respectful and be on your absolute best behavior, OK?" They both nodded their heads and responded in a hushed tone, "Yes, Mom!" And then Izzy asked, "This is where Otto Frank went to prison, right, Mom?" I was floored. Kayla looked at me with giant eyes and said, "Izzy, you are so stinking smart!"

This moment was just one of the many reasons I chose to travel with my kids. This moment was the reason I would bring them to a place like this, the reason Brian and I made these experiences a priority over family trips to theme parks or tanning on a tourist-laden beach somewhere. My four-year-old daughter, at the entrance of the Auschwitz concentration camp, had connected that Otto Frank was Anne Frank's dad—something we just learned in Amsterdam—and was imprisoned in this exact spot before he was released and went on to publish his daughter's diary. It was an incredible moment. Her curiosity and understanding were a beautiful thing to experience and encouraged me to provide her with more. As trivial as it may sound, that moment made me so unbelievably proud to be her mom, to be a part of her education, to witness her make this connection and take in a piece of information she'll never forget. This alone was enough for me to be comfortable bringing my kids inside the prison walls. I knew they wouldn't understand most of it, but they were mature and well-behaved enough to handle themselves, and when they got tired or it got to be too much, we would make our way back.

As we approached the entrance, I slowed my pace and took in the sight before me. *Arbeit Macht Frei*—"work will set you free"—in big block letters, looming over the wrought iron entrance gate of the death camp. I had seen these same words and felt this same wave of nausea wash over me as I had walked through the gates of Sachsenhausen concentration camp in Germany a few years prior, but I hadn't fully prepared myself for the moment when I'd walk through the gate of Auschwitz, knowing full well that more than one million people walked through this gate before me, looked up at these same words, *Arbeit Macht Frei*, and never made it back out. It was a haunting feeling and one that has stayed with me since.

Our tour guide led us through the gate, past a row of brick buildings (referred to as blocks), all with numbers on the outside and each block having served a different purpose during the camp's operational years (1940-1945). The orderly brick structures looked as innocent as classroom buildings on any high school or college campus in small-town U.S.A., which made their true purpose even more unbelievable and horrific. We toured a medical ward where indescribable, inhuman experiments had been conducted, a prison ward for non-Jewish offenders awaiting execution, and an administrative office where prisoners were assigned striped pajamas and identification numbers. We saw photos and heard stories of the trains arriving, the SS separating families—men to the left, women and children to the right—and walked through a gas chamber and the crematorium next door. The rooms were dark. Twists and turns of a hallway led to a room with cement floors, walls and ceiling, with no windows or air flowing through it. The air was stale and it was impossible to escape the understanding that horrible atrocities had been committed here. Prisoners were only given a cup of water, a scant half cup of soup for lunch, and about ten ounces of bread for dinner. Prisoners who stepped on a certain cobblestone pathway within the camp were immediately executed. Discovering these facts, these living—and dying—conditions was nearly unbearable. We took in our surroundings, closing our eyes and visualizing the unimaginable that happened where we were now standing. And then we walked through the human remains room.

I lost it.

I couldn't stop the tears. I was using my sleeve to wipe them from my cheek, but they just kept coming. Human hair. Two tons of it. Blonde, brown, gray, some still braided, some unraveled, some fashioned into hairnets or woven into fabric. We were looking at the hair of people no different than the six of us, all who had walked through that same gate we just had, all in different stages, phases, places of their lives, but who all had died there. It was unreal. Devastating, sad, haunting, life-changing. Incomprehensible. There were no words to describe how excruciating it was to witness and recognize exactly what we were looking at.

The suitcases came next. A handful of them were marked with names and birthdates, carefully written before being packed with their owners' most prized possessions. Brown, black, leather, some with straps, some handles, some lined with fabric, all with only one thing in common: they belonged to people who carried them from their homes onto the trains that brought them to this place; this horrific, haunted, evil place...assuming they'd be reunited with these humble belongings once the war ended. Again, unreal. Except it was not. I turned to Kayla, who sobbed softly and Kasey, who was trying her best to hold back her tears. Adeline was asleep in her carrier on my back, so I held Hudson's hand a little tighter and we continued on.

We eventually walked through one of the housing blocks and saw the three-tier wooden bunk beds. Picturing twenty people trying to sleep on each of these beds with rats and mice scampering around them...each person so unbelievably hungry and desperate—these were pictures I'd seen in my history book—but now I was staring at them face to face with my children and friends next to me. I thought of the moms just like me, holding their children, begging for food, for a scrap, a morsel of something—anything—and being powerless to help, and how unbearable it would be to hear my own children cry out in hunger. The pain and sadness in these thoughts alone was palpable even eight decades later. Picturing guards coming to work every day and hearing the kids cry, seeing these babies starving before their very eyes, how did they live with themselves? Going home to their own families, sitting down at their dinner table knowing what was happening behind these gates. I looked down at Izzy and Hudson and I felt Adeline, and shook my head, using my already damp sleeve to wipe away the fresh set of tears from my eyes.

We spent three hours touring Auschwitz, the last two of which we'd spent sharing umbrellas and dodging mud puddles as the gloomy grey sky finally burst open and started pouring down rain on us. It was an uncanny—but fitting—way to experience what can only be described as one of the most depressing places on Earth, and I think we were all relieved when our tour came to an end. We were walking toward the same gate we'd entered through, *Arbeit Mach Frei*, now in view—this time in reverse—heading down the gravel road toward our van, all lost in our own thoughts, when a white-haired woman approached us.

"The best way to prevent something like this from ever happening again is to start with you kids." She said, looking directly from Isabel to Hudson.

Izzy grabbed Kayla's hand a little tighter, unsure who this woman was or why she was suddenly walking next to us.

"This is a really special experience for you kids," she continued in what I assumed was a Scandinavian-ish accent. "It's important for you to know what happened here, so that you don't ever let it happen again. Bless your little children and you, too, mama, for bringing them here."

I didn't need the confirmation that it was okay for me to bring my children there; they had behaved perfectly, asked important questions, looked at what they found interesting, and away from what they didn't. I knew by bringing them here, I was offering them an experience that many parents can't—or won't—provide their own kids, and I knew they would be better for it, but this complete stranger's words were the validation I needed.

As the kids slept and the adults sat in silence, we drove back to Warsaw. I began pondering...why, in my current state of trying to heal, of trying to grieve my own sadness, my own loss, would I choose to go to a place of such devastation? It was a valid question. I was sure many would not choose to do this, to put themselves in a position knowing the despair they would feel walking into a place of such horrific sadness. I felt quite the opposite, actually. I wanted to expose myself to sadness, to open myself to grief, and to let myself feel everything I had to feel.

Experiencing emotions makes me feel human and lets me know I am living. Hearing Izzy thinking out loud as she connected the dots of the historical events she'd been witnessing and learning about during our trip made it all worth it for me.

Despite all of the sadness, I also felt so incredibly humbled and grateful that these gates were open to us, to allow people from around the world to visit and grieve and mourn and ask questions. It's such an incredible opportunity for growth and learning for people of all ages.

Four hours—and one emergency car-sick stop—later, we parted ways with our faithful driver, who thanked us and asked: "So, where are you going next?"

Chapter Fourteen

"Is this Switzerland?" Hudson's sugary sweet voice floated up from his place next to me. He was holding my hand tightly, proud to be walking next to his momma as we made our way through the Zürich airport, the luxury and decadence of the shops we walked past doing their best to lure us in, pleading with us to spend money before we'd even left the international concourse.

"This is Switzerland, bud!" I smiled back at him, offering his hand a tight squeeze as we found our way to the baggage claim.

Wow, Switzerland. I can't believe I'm here.

"Uggghhh I'm sticky!" Izzy cried out as we stepped outside, immediately confronted with a brutal dose of summer heat and humidity. "It's too hot here!"

We loaded up our rental car, turned the air conditioner on as high as it went, and hit the road. Destination: A one-hundred-year-old farmhouse located outside the city limits in a town called St. Gallen. We spent the next ninety minutes traversing

single lane roads, marveling at the vast farmland and beautiful mountains surrounding us, a scene as picturesque as you'd
imagine if you were to close your eyes and think of Switzerland.

"Look at the sheep!" Kayla pointed out her window to Hudson.

"I see them, Kay!" Hudson yelled as he pressed his forehead
against the window to get a better view.

Our GPS was soon blinking, telling us we were close, but the
streets were all unmarked, and the houses—with no numbers—
were known by the locals as "the *Haus Buelenhof*" and "Paul's
place" as we soon realized upon stopping to ask for directions.
We did eventually arrive, only to find the door unlocked as we
were immediately engulfed with a deep, rich smell of "old" as
we opened the heavy wooden door. We walked through the doorway and took in our surroundings, wooden stairs made from raw
lumber—planks older than my grandpa—leading up the stairs to
a series of hallways, which led to more stairs and more hallways.
This house was huge, furnished entirely in deep maroon velvet
furniture and white lace accents, full of antiques that I'm sure
had been in the home from the time it was built. Kasey, Kayla,
and I thought it was beautiful. Isabel hated it.

"What's the matter, sweetheart?" I asked, pulling Izzy into
my arms.

"I don't want to have my birthday in this smelly old farmhouse!" she declared indignantly with a hearty foot stomp to let
me know she was serious. She knew we'd be celebrating her
fifth birthday in Switzerland and apparently this ancient venue
was not what she'd had in mind for the festivities.

The house didn't have any modern luxuries. It was located
on a working farm and we could engage with the family farm

animals—alpaca, horses, and a goat named Django—and the backyard had a breathtaking view of the mountains surrounding us. It was a stunning and purely Swiss experience. The owners came over to introduce themselves and we learned that the seventy-year-old man named Paul was actually born in the house, had lived there most of his life, and now lived in the house next door.

While Kayla and Kasey settled down with the kids, I began searching the internet for local bakeries that could deliver a cake. I finally found one and made the phone call.

"For how many people?" the lady asked.

"Well, it's six of us—we're traveling from the United States and it's my daughter's fifth birthday, I'd like to do something special for her."

"We make cakes for a minimum of ten people," the lady quickly specified, interrupting me.

"Oh, OK," I said. "That will work."

"What would you like for decorations?"

"Well..." I thought of Izzy, who was still mopey, and felt my heart shrink. I knew she was excited about her upcoming birthday and without the luxuries of home, needed to do what I could to make it special for her "My daughter loves the Disney movie *Frozen*, if you could use that as a theme?" I asked.

We ended the conversation, and I was soon onto my next task of finding a place where I could buy party supplies. *I miss Target!* I thought to myself while coming to terms with the reality that finding a party supply store in the middle of the Swiss countryside was certainly not going to be easy. *Maybe I could order them online and have them delivered?* Nope. *Dangit.*

Maybe the cake lady would know where to find some and be able to bring them with the cake? Kasey and Kayla laughed at that idea. *Maybe our seventy-year-old Airbnb host would have a line on some Frozen themed birthday party decorations?* Hmm. *It was worth a try.*

"Guys! We have to go!" I yelled to everyone currently scattered throughout the house. "Jessica's train will be here in thirty minutes!" My sister Jessica was flying in from Seattle, Washington, and we headed to the train station to grab her to join us for a few days of adventure, and Isabel's birthday celebration.

"Mommmmm! I can't find my shoes!" Hudson yelled from the top of the stairs.

You'd think after four weeks of traveling together, we'd have some sort of system down where at least everybody knew where their own shoes were, and yet there we were, over five thousand miles from our house, but still dealing with the same daily struggles we did at home.

"Kasey, do you have Hudson's shoes?" I yelled toward the kitchen.

"Yep! Be right there." Kasey responded, busy with packing sandwiches and snacks for the day.

An hour later, with Jessica secured from the train station, we were back on the road, this time winding uphill, traversing the hairpin turns of the mountain, through small villages whose roads were made of stone so bumpy our cheeks jiggled as we drove over them.

"We're here!!" I finally announced, louder than necessary, to my travel companions who had fallen asleep on the two-hour drive to our destination. "Hey…check this out!"

We had just arrived at Rhine Falls—Europe's largest waterfall—and after winding down the steeper and longer-than-expected pathway from the parking lot, we were treated to sweeping views of the river pouring in from the mountains around us. It was a magnificent sight only compounded by the thunderous sound of the rushing falls.

"Woah! It's breathtaking!" Kayla shouted from her place next to me on the viewing platform. It really was a beautiful sight, the river converging in multiple spots before combining in one powerful burst as it hurled itself over the rocks and into the stunning waterfall in front of us. We eventually walked the rest of the way down the mountain, crossing the frigid river before making our way to the boat platform for a ride into the falls. We paid our 15 Euros each and spent the rest of the afternoon laughing and enjoying the reprieve from the heat as we got sprayed and splashed with the icy cold water. With my kids and closest friends next to me, and in a moment of happiness and celebration, I scattered some of Brian's ashes right there from our boat, knowing he'd have delighted in this experience as well.

"Momma, can we get an ice cream?" Izzy asked as we stepped off the boat that had conveniently docked right in front of an ice cream stand.

"Sure, kiddo." It was too hot to argue, and the kids had been such troopers in the heat. We spent the next hour taking turns sitting in the only patch of shade we could find, as the kids enjoyed an ice cream cone and the adults enjoyed a cold-ish glass of wine, savoring our last views of the Falls. Soon enough it was time to pack up and head back to the farmhouse to meet the baker who'd be delivering Izzy's cake—apparently understanding the instructions to deliver to "Paul's farmhouse" in St. Gallen. Two hours later we pulled into the driveway of our rented home just in time for the baker to pull up behind us. I ushered everyone across the street to the park so Izzy wouldn't see the cake before her birthday the next morning.

"Oh my gosh, it's beautiful!" I gushed as she opened the large white box revealing the three-tiered *Frozen* themed birthday cake. How much do I owe you?" I asked her.

"It'll be $240."

I blinked and adjusted my body to better accommodate the box of decorated sugar, eggs, and flour in my arms. *There's no way I heard that correctly. Maybe it was a confusion with the currency exchange?*

"You said $240?" I asked, just to be sure. "Is that U.S. $240?"

"Yes."

Yikes. This is a lot of money where I come from! In fact, this was more than the plane ticket to get us to Switzerland in the first place! I knew Switzerland was expensive, but $240 for a cake!? Ouch. I wasn't prepared for that. Why didn't I think to ask how much it would be before this?

"The baker said this needs to be refrigerated overnight, but the cake won't fit!" I told Kasey as she walked in, having come back to get some water, but now wondering what I was doing, trying to shove the giant white box in the tiny farmhouse refrigerator. After multiple attempts of shuffling things around, I surrendered, and set the cake, still in the box, on the table.

"Oh well," I said, more to myself than to Kasey who had watched the entire comical scene unfold. "It's only for the night, I'm sure it will be fine."

Once the sun set and the kids had all gone to bed, Jessica, Kasey, Kayla, and I set up the few birthday decorations I'd been able to collect during our past few weeks of traveling. Streamers of various colors hung from antique lamps, handmade cards adorned the table full of small gifts I'd packed in my backpack, and a large white birthday cake box perched precariously on the edge of the table, waiting for its big reveal to the birthday girl.

The next morning, the sun's rays pierced through the red velvet curtains and the house began to stir. "This is the best day ever!" Izzy shouted the moment she walked down the wooden staircase and saw the decorations, her sleep-filled eyes now full of wonder and excitement. She walked through the kitchen entryway with a giant smile on her face, soaking up the attention and savoring the experience of waking up to her fifth birthday in Switzerland with all of her favorite people surrounding her, at some point having come around to accept, then embrace this "smelly old farmhouse." We exploded in a chorus of "Happy Birthday dear Izzy" before each offering her big hugs and birthday wishes. I gave her an extra-long hug, not believing my sweet little Isabel was somehow now five! It had been five years since Brian and I had been in that hospital room, since we'd held hands and brought this spunky, beautiful, hilarious little girl into the world. I held her tight and smiled, her messy blonde hair tickling my face as I savored the moment.

"Do you want to see your cake?" I whispered into her ear, excited to show her the $240 treasure I'd had delivered the day before.

"Yessss!" she shouted as she wriggled free from my arms.

"I have a surprise for you," I told her. "We are going to call everybody back home, so they can be part of your birthday party as well!" I quickly logged on Facebook and started my live feed, which many of our family members and friends began watching—despite the nine-hour time difference between Oregon and Switzerland.

We sent our love to everybody from the farmhouse as people from around the world wished Izzy a happy birthday and I handed the phone to Kasey so she could record the big reveal of the birthday cake as Izzy got to see it for the first time.

"Are you ready?" I asked Isabel, and the hordes of people now watching.

Izzy screamed, "Yes!" and clapped her hands with joy.

"Happy birthd—" *Oh noooo!* As soon as I had the lid off of the white box and saw what happened, my jaw dropped. *What the...* What was a gorgeous birthday cake last night was now a mash of sugar, flour, and eggs resting in a pool of melted light blue and purple buttercream frosting. I had left the cake on the table overnight and it had completely disintegrated, melting beyond recognition.

"Mom!" Izzy cried, tears immediately in her eyes, her disappointment palpable.

"Honey, I'm so sorry!" I said, trying to shake off my own disappointment. I looked up hoping to find support from my friends, when I saw the phone still in Kasey's hand, quickly reminding me we were live on Facebook and a whole bunch of people had just witnessed what I considered one of my biggest—or at least most public—mom failures. *Whoops.* I shifted the heavy box slightly in my hands, a glimmer from one of the *Frozen* characters that once decorated the beautiful cake, but now laid in a pile of rubble contained in this cake box, cast a shadow across Izzy's disappointed face. *I promise, it was a cool cake, Iz.* I spent the rest of the day trying to make it up to her, though I'm sure I will likely never hear the end of that one.

I wish I could say that was my last—we'll call it a blunder—in Switzerland, but I can't. A few days after the melted-birthday-cake debacle, we dropped Jessica off at the train station to fly home and left Zürich to spend a few days exploring southern Switzerland. We were particularly excited to spend a few days in Zermatt, the nearly mile-high mountain resort. It was a full day of travel to get there, and we had plans to stop along the way to see a few sights and even visit with Chris, a friend of Brian's from Hawaii who just happened to be in town. Brian and Chris has bonded while diving the reefs of Honolulu; Chris an accomplished underwater photographer, and Brian aspiring to become one. Chris could often be found at the Haleiwa Art Gallery, standing proudly next to one of his colorful images in his equally colorful Hawaiian print shirts, and Brian could often be found asking me to pull the car over on our family outings up to the North Shore so he could run inside "real quick" to say hi and see Chris' latest capture. Brian looked up to Chris and was inspired by his artwork.

"Does everyone have everything?" I shouted up the stairs as I finished loading the car. "Kids? Baby Bear? Pink blanket?"

"Yes, we're good!" Kayla shouted back.

Next to our passports and my credit card, the only real necessities of this trip were Isabel's pink blanket she'd had since she was born, and Baby Bear, Hudson's favorite stuffed animal that never, ever, left his side.

We left Zürich at 5:30 a.m. and drove two hours south to the town of Interlaken where we met up with Chris. Our trip had already been full of highlights and incredible moments but meeting a friend of Brian's—somebody I'd never met in person but had heard stories about, in the middle of the Bernese Alps—was truly special.

"I used to live right over there!" Chris pointed out the window of our train, excited to be making this connection with Hudson and Isabel.

"Mom, I see snow!" Isabel exclaimed as we crept higher and higher up the mountain, it's snow-capped peaks suddenly visible.

"Oh my… we might be a little underdressed for this." I laughed and simultaneously cringed as I looked down at my own shorts and T-shirt, the kids in their sandals and shorts.

We were headed for *Jungfraujoch*, the "Top of Europe," the highest train station in Europe, but in our haste to leave the farm-house that morning, we hadn't planned our outfits well for the day. It had been in the nineties all week in Zürich and we hadn't set aside any cold-weather gear for this specific leg of our trip.

"We can buy sweatshirts at the gift shop if we need to." I reassured my crew, now looking at me for reassurance.

Our train eventually ground to a stop at *Jungfraujoch* or the "maiden saddle" of ice that connects one mountain range to another in the Bernese Alps and the end of the train ride. We stepped off the train and were immediately rewarded with sweeping views of the glaciers and mountains all around us, a sight straight out of a fairy tale. We were at the "Top of Europe" and it felt like it. The sun was shining, reflecting off the snow and ice all around us and it was stunning. People were sledding, ziplining and climbing, and there was a little hut where weary adventurers could buy hot chocolate and champagne. We spent the next few hours—completely under-dressed for the occasion—indulging in both while having snowball fights, taking photos, and making memories.

In every photo taken of Hudson, Baby Bear was slung across his shoulder or dangling precariously from his hand, trudging through the snow, and taking in the sights with him, sitting in his lap on the train rides up and then again on the way back down the mountain. Baby Bear was with us as we said goodbye to Chris, and then kept Hudson's neck propped up as he napped, and we continued on with our three-hour drive down to Zermatt.

"We're almost there, guys!" I said as the town of Zermatt came into view. The six of us had just put in a fourteen-hour day of traveling—traversing Switzerland north to south, by train, car, foot, a strange train/car/pitch black tunnel excursion we weren't expecting, and other various modes of transportation. Needless to say, we were exhausted. "You guys! Wake up!"

Zermatt was a car-free town, so we parked our rental car at the train terminal and grabbed our luggage. Kasey woke up all three kids and we grabbed a taxi that brought us to the border of Zermatt and then hired an electric car to take us to our hotel. It had been a long day. I reserved two hotel rooms—Kayla, Kasey, and Hudson in one room, and Izzy, Adeline, and myself in another. After checking in, we walked around town in search of a cold soda and a few snacks to get us through the night, and then we went back to our hotel, ready for sleep. *Goodnight, you guys. See you in the morning!*

"Do you have Baby Bear?" Kayla texted me, not five minutes after I'd said goodnight and closed the door to my own hotel room.

No way! My heart stopped. *Baby Bear!*

***

"Babe!" Brian yelled up the stairs to get my attention. I was six months pregnant and Brian would be diving all weekend, so we'd reached a compromise that he'd take the kids with him for the afternoon to give me a little break at home. I had helped load the kids into the car on their way out, carefully placing Baby Bear in Hudson's lap and giving them both kisses before closing the door. I watched them back out of the driveway, on their way to a day full of adventure.

"Babe!" Brian called up the stairs again later that afternoon upon their return home. "Have you seen Baby Bear?"

"Hudson had him when you left! Did you check the car?" I called back from my place in the bathtub..

"Oh no…" Brian responded. I didn't have to see the look on his face to know the look of fear that was currently occupying it.

Hudson hadn't slept a single night of his life without that stuffed bear by his side. This would be bad.

"Did you check the car? I asked.

"Yeah…oh no babe. I think we might have left if at the dive shop." Brian responded. He tried calling the dive shop, and then the individual divers he'd seen there in case anyone was still at the shop and could let him in to pick up Hudson's stuffed bear. No luck. This was a rough night of sleep for all of us, but Brian

raced to the dive shop early the next morning, retrieving baby bear and reuniting him with his best friend. This was the only night of Hudson's life he had slept without this bear. Until now.

***

I didn't have him. Hudson didn't have him. Kayla and Kasey didn't have him.

And then it hit me: We'd left Baby Bear in the car.

I could hear Hudson crying from their hotel room right above me. I checked the clock: 10:00 p.m. *Ughhhh.* I was so excruciatingly tired and simply didn't have it in me to walk to the train station, take the train to the car, get the stuffed bear, and come back.

"Oh nooo...I think we left him in the car," I wrote back.

"No worries, I got this," Kayla responded.

Twenty minutes later my phone went off again, this time a photo of Kayla snuggled up in bed next to Hudson, his arm thrown around her neck like he did his bear, sound asleep. Thanks to Kayla, we made it through the night, but not without a solid heap of mom-guilt for forgetting it in the first place.

I woke up with the sun the next morning and was on the first shuttle back to the parking garage to retrieve Baby Bear. A $16 train ticket was the price of happiness when it came to a three-year-old being reunited with his best friend. And what a sweet reunion it was. Once that crisis was settled, we were ready for the day's adventure. We boarded yet another train, this one bound for Sunnegga, located just outside the town of Zermatt, which was supposed to be a great place to view the Matterhorn—a 14,000-foot-tall mountain in the Swiss Alps, and the crown jewel of Zermatt and surrounds.

"Addy, look at the mountain!" I gasped as it came into view. I couldn't be sure if her senses were taking in the beauty around us or if she was doing anything other than looking straight ahead or if she'd even remember any of this experience. I know there are amazing children who remember memories from very young ages...some even before they can speak...and I wondered this about my baby. Would it happen? Could it happen? I'd like to think that on a cellular level, on a soul level, that Addy knew something special was happening. Only time would tell. We'd experienced our first sighting the night before while walking the streets of Zermatt in search of snacks, the hat-shaped mountain towering above and beckoning out from every street corner of town. But, as we walked off the train, down and around a bend in the trail, there she was: the world-famous Matterhorn in all of her iconic beauty. I grew up in the Pacific Northwest, surrounded by stunning landscapes and gorgeous mountains, but this—the Matterhorn standing right in front of me—was a sight like nothing I had ever seen before.

"You guys. This is unreal." I said to nobody in particular. We were all wrapped up in our own thoughts, the vision of this mountain in front of us suddenly overwhelming each of us in our own way.

"Mom, this is boringggg!" Izzy's voice cut through the moment.

"Haha, OK sweetheart, let's go." I laughed.

It wasn't boring though. Seeing the Matterhorn for the first time in my life was an emotional experience.

"Mom! Hudson's looking at me!" Izzy cried, her voice ringing out.

"No, I'm not!" Hudson yelled back, reaching out to hit his sister in retaliation.

"Both of you, knock it off!" I said in the sternest mom voice I could muster.

This is too much.

There we were in the middle of the Swiss Alps, this iconic mountain in front of us, images of men and women who had tried—and failed—to climb her throughout the years now flooding my thoughts, knowing what generations of explorers who stood in this very spot before me had felt while looking at her. I knew I was going to cry. I could taste it in my throat, I could feel it in my eyes. My nostrils started burning like they do when you try to do a somersault in the pool and forget to hold your nose.

"Can you take the kids to get lunch?" I asked as we approached the crest of the path we were on. "I just need a minute."

"Take your time." Kasey responded, seeing that I was fighting back tears.

Content with the fact Izzy, Hudson, and Adeline were safe with Kasey and Kayla, I grabbed the opportunity for some private time. I walked down the hill adjacent of the gondola we'd just walked off and sat on a patch of grass facing the Matterhorn. I took a deep breath and finally allowed the tears to come. I thought of those who had been there before me, taking in the sight of this magnificent mountain, looking at this natural wonder and routing out their plan to climb it, to conquer it, and with it…whether they succeeded or not… leaving behind a piece of themselves. I could feel the pull of the mountain, the allure, the draw of wanting to feel a part of it. I understood the desire to want to be a part of something bigger than yourself. To push yourself and see if you could do it. The heart of an explorer.

I miss him.

I knew what it felt like to be drawn to something. When you have this sense of adventure inside of you, it's impossible to ignore or to pretend it doesn't exist. Not everybody understands, but I do. I might not personally have felt the intense desire to ascend the Matterhorn, but I understand those who did. And Brian would have too. There are always risks involved, but those who understand, know it would be scarier to die without ever having lived, without ever having questioned and experienced, than to die doing something that brings joy to your life.

I understand, Brian. I miss you so much, but I understand.

Sitting at the base of the Matterhorn, I paid my respects to the men and women who understood the risks, took them anyway, and didn't make it home to tell their stories. A few hours earlier, we had walked through the cemetery in town that hosted the headstones—and the names—of those who didn't make it back from climbing this mountain in front of me. Some of the headstones even carried the exact locations where they perished, which somehow made it that much more real—they were sons, husbands, daughters, sisters, and they would never return back home to their loved ones. The mountain had claimed them. One headstone in particular stood out amongst the rest: Donald Stephen Williams. "I chose to climb" inscribed across the front. I never met this young man who was born in 1958. He died in 1975, before I was even born—but these words resonated so strongly with me. He died climbing the Matterhorn, chasing after a dream, a vision, a yearning. He died while truly living and that's more than some ever get the chance to say. *I hope someday, somebody walks past my headstone long after I'm gone and is able to say the same thing.* While sitting in front of the mountain, I took a few deep breaths to help regulate my heart rate, I closed my eyes, and whispered, "Cheers to you, Donald Stephen Williams. You're inspiring people even after all these years. I hope you know that. Rest easy."

I opened my eyes and smiled, thinking of Brian. He just wanted to enjoy life, to enjoy these experiences, to push himself and prove to himself that he could do it. I knew the men and women who didn't make it back from this mountain felt that same feeling inside of them, and just like Brian, even in death, they were encouraging others to do the same.

In the presence of the Matterhorn, this grand dame of mountains, it was impossible to ignore how insanely beautiful it was, and just how small it made me feel. Seeing it in front of me and viewing her through the lens of an explorer did not make me want to climb it, but it did make me want to conquer other things. It compelled me to support and encourage those around me to pursue their passions, to chase after their dreams, to climb mountains—literally and figuratively. It made me want to push myself to continue to do the same. I allowed myself to feel and mourn and celebrate, to question and to think, to dream and to plan. The experience changed me. It encouraged and inspired me, and I know that, regardless of the obstacles and challenges in front of me, I will keep climbing and I will make it to the top or I will die trying. I'm at peace with that thought.

I walked back to meet with Kayla, Kasey, and my children. My eyes were red and puffy from crying, but I had a bright, genuine smile on my face as my children—with Baby Bear in tow—greeted me with love as only children can. With utter, unabashed joy.

We will make it. I'm more positive in this moment than any other prior moment.

Chapter Fifteen

This is Greece? I wondered silently as our hired van turned left and then right down the graffiti-laden streets of Athens. The shops were reinforced with steel bars on their windows, and rubbish littered the spots where the shop gates met the crumbling cement sidewalks. Blue and white lights flickering above what I imagined were once bustling stores—they were now abandoned, the illuminated signs now only a symbol of what once was.

This wasn't the Greece from the postcards and nature documentaries I'd grown up watching. "So…this isn't quite what I'd pictured Greece would look like," I said. I was careful to keep my first impression to myself, as I didn't want to offend our local driver by making any potentially rude or unsavory comments.

"Ewww, mama! That guy is peeing!" Isabel pointed out her window and began laughing hysterically as we stopped at a red light and were treated to the sight of a homeless man relieving himself into a shrub.

I was doing my very best to make sure we all had fun and soaked in as much quality time and curated sightseeing as we could, all while keeping the overall mission true to its core and to our hearts. Remember. Laugh. Cry. Love. Heal. I wanted to plan but I also wanted us to go with the flow and discover sights, sounds, tastes, and feelings off the beaten path. From our initial views of Greece, somehow a whirlwind tour wasn't looking that bad at this point.

Kayla, Kasey, and I couldn't help but laugh at the situation, doing our best to distract the kids and ourselves from our own unmet expectations of Athens. Greece had been one of the places we had been most excited to visit, and when I booked this specific leg of our itinerary, I pictured deep blue water set against the bright white buildings, ancient Greek ruins, Mediterranean natives with olive skin dressed in white linen clothes and woven fishermen's sandals lunching at outdoor cafes, all of the things that represented this part of the world to me. Never once in my visions of Greece and all that we'd get to see and experience there, did a homeless man relieving himself outside our van window just one hour after arriving in the country, come to mind.

"Here you go," our driver announced as he pulled our over-sized van onto the sidewalk—certainly impeding foot traffic in the process. "You're over there." He pointed to a graffiti-covered four-story building across the street. There were bars on all the first-floor windows, a locked gate out front, and a few suspicious looking loiterers standing outside the entryway. *Yikes.*

"Okay guys, home sweet home!" I smiled, trying to make light of this unexpected and somewhat uncomfortable scenario. Kayla and Kasey cringed, their eyebrows furrowed as if to ask if this was for real. "We'll laugh about this someday!" I said, already laughing to myself. I'd lived in big cities around the United States, and while I hadn't necessarily expected Athens to look like this, these sights were nothing new to me. We unloaded and made our way up to the apartment.

Kayla exclaimed "This space is so light!" as she made her way through the apartment. We followed her through each room, marveling at how beautiful the inside of this historic building really was: the kitchen counters were made of solid marble, the floors were pristine hardwood, and there was an amazing panoramic wall of windows leading out to a balcony where we could take in sights of the chaos below us. The inside of this building certainly didn't match the outside, and this was the little boost we needed to feel comfortable settling in for the night.

The light filtered in through the large bay windows early the next morning, waking us from our first night in Greece. "You guys! We're going to see the Parthenon today!" I yelled across the apartment, still cozy in bed, but anxious for everyone to wake up so we could head out for the day. A symbol of ancient Greece, and one of the most iconic and historic landmarks in the world, the Parthenon is a piece of history that everyone has read about and today, we'd get to see it with our own eyes. *Izzy, Hudson, Addy, you guys are so lucky. You'll study this someday, too, and I'll show you the photos of you standing here, witnessing it for yourself.*

"OK," our driver announced twenty minutes after we squeezed ourselves into his car, "here we are!"

I looked around but didn't see anything resembling the Greek ruins from my history textbooks. "Where is the Parthenon?" I asked him.

"It's up there," he said, pointing his finger up the hill in front of us. "You just have to walk."

"Ahh OK! You guys ready?" I asked everyone as they craned their necks to see how far we would need to walk.

"Ughh, it's too hot!!" Izzy was the first to complain. She was right, it was very hot. We had thought Switzerland was warm, but this was probably the most extreme heat any of us had ever experienced before, this trip or otherwise. We'd been outside of the air conditioned van for less than a minute and we were already sweaty.

"OK, let's go guys! Let's see it and then we can get some water and maybe an ice cream cone!" I tried to sound as enthusiastic as possible, but even I was uncomfortable in this excessive heat.

"Whoa!" I said, trying to catch my balance as my open-toe sandals came in contact with the very first marble step leading up to the temple. "Careful you guys!" I shouted down to my friends and kids below me. "It's really slippery!" Kayla and Kasey were trying to carry Addy—still in her stroller—up these steep, slippery steps, as Hudson and Isabel watched them with concern, hoping they wouldn't drop the stroller and its contents on them during this hike. It was a scene from a comedy show— we were completely unprepared for the heat as we hiked up this hill, completely overwhelmed by the hordes of people surrounding us, and concerned about navigating slippery marble steps with a baby in a stroller. All we could do was laugh at ourselves and keep marching. In the heat. Did I mention it was excruciatingly hot?

"Ice cream!!" Hudson shouted, the first to see the familiar photo of the cold treat—an iconic image of its own to kids around the world—as he and Izzy broke free from the pack and ran toward it. "Can we get some!?"

"Of course!" I smiled, knowing we'd need water too. *How can any place on Earth be this frigging hot?*

We walked closer, looking forward to quenching our thirst and regaining some energy.

"Sorry, no water," said the lady behind the stand.

"I'm sorry?" *I must have misunderstood.* I made the best "water bottle" gesture I could think of, asking again, "Water?"

"No." She replied again. *OK, I didn't misunderstand.* We were out of luck. "Ice cream?" I asked, knowing the kids wouldn't understand if they didn't have any.

"No." I heard the familiar word again. I had to laugh at this point.

"OK, um...juice?" I asked again, my voice full of hope.

"This or this?" I interpreted her thick Greek accent to be saying as she pointed back and forth between an orange and then purple slushy concoction.

"I'll take five," I said, deciding on the orange one, paying my bill, and walking toward the group I'd left under the only patch of shade we'd found in the vicinity.

"Mama! That's not ice cream!" I heard first, soon followed by, "No. I don't want that!"

"This is all they had, guys!" I looked from Kasey to Kayla for support as they looked back at me with eyes that said, "What the..., Ash, where's the water?"

This was turning into a nightmare. We each took a sip of the orange drink, deciding it was too sweet—even for the kids—and too hot, so we quickly decided just to power through, climb the rest of the way up the hill, see the ruins, take some photos, and head back to the comfort of our air conditioned apartment.

"Watch out!" Kayla yelled as EMTs rushed past us to evacuate a woman who had been overcome by heat stroke. We'd made it up the hill, posed for a few photos, captured the memory and the experience, but this was crazy, and potentially unsafe for the kids if I kept them out in this heat much longer. *Time to go.*

"Alright, let's get out of here," I said, exhausted from the heat and lack of water, but happy we had made it to the top of the hill to see the Parthenon, to know what Acropolis looks like, what the surrounding areas felt and smelled like. *I won't need to come back anytime soon.*

The walk down the hill was much smoother and less intense, and we all rejoiced when we got in the car.

"Welcome back," our driver greeted us. "Are you hungry?"

He took us to a restaurant near our apartment in downtown Athens and we gorged on feta cheese, roasted veggies, fresh bread, salad drizzled with fresh olive oil and, you guessed it, lots of water! This was the best meal we'd had since starting this journey across the globe, and it was well worth the wait. The handsome young waiters with their olive skin and dark features who fussed over the kids and brought us free dessert kept Kasey and Kayla as enthralled as the kids. *Maybe Athens wasn't so bad after all.* We made a standing reservation at this restaurant for our remaining nights in town and gained no fewer than five pounds each because of it. To this day I daydream of its deep fried feta cheese encased in buttery layers of phyllo dough with honey drizzled on top.

We spent the next few days exploring different areas of Athens, usually only for an hour or two at a time before retreating back to the apartment to cool down. Europe was experiencing a heat wave and Athens had been hit hard. We used this time to rest, recharge, watch movies, and play games. The kids were happy to have a few days of downtime and undivided attention as we recounted stories of things we'd experienced on the trip so far. Soon enough, our time in Athens had come to an end, and our van driver was back outside our apartment, parked in "his spot" on the sidewalk—this time at 5 a.m.—and we watched in fascination as the nightclubs lining the street outside our apartment slowly began to close down for the night as we carried three half-asleep children across the street, loading up our bags to head to the airport, again. This next flight would keep us in the country of Greece, but take us south to the island of Santorini, located in the Aegean Sea.

"Two months, seven countries." The sign welcoming our crew to the beautiful Greek island was unmistakable. The fact it was held by a 5-foot, 7-inch tall , Greek man wearing a T-shirt and pair of jean shorts was comical. I'm not sure exactly what this man holding the sign was expecting "two months, seven countries" to look like as it spilled out of the baggage claim at the tiny Santorini airport, but the look on his face as the six of us approached him, certainly gave away that it wasn't us.

"Just you?" He asked, obviously looking for any male companions we might have with us.

"Yep, just us!" We smiled back at him. We'd been through this before, the question didn't even phase us at this point. *We're here! This is the Greece I've seen in photos.* The bluest of blue in the ocean, the bright white domes of houses and churches set on the cliffs over the water below. *This is unbelievable.*

"You guys," I said.

"I know!" Kasey and Kayla responded in unison, as our driver wound the nine-passenger van through the unmarked streets of the island, headed toward our home. I hadn't planned much for our time in Santorini, outside of spending as much time on the water as possible.

Before we'd left the United States on this journey, I spoke to a filmmaker friend from home, Brae Hunziker, who also happened to be spending his summer in Europe. I'd asked him to meet us in Santorini and travel around for the few weeks following this stop to capture some footage of our adventure—a documentary of sorts—so we'd have it to look back on later to relive some of these memories. Besides meeting up with Brae, and Adeline celebrating her first birthday, we'd be able to spend our time relaxing on the beach and taking in the sights.

I had known Brae for a few years before inviting him on this trip, having hired him for a couple of film projects, and then to document Brian's transpacific sailing adventure. Despite all of the talking, texting, and time spent together on these projects, I really didn't know much about him on a personal level. However, in a late night, heartfelt conversation, I'd learned that Brae lost his own mother, Terri, to cancer when he was only eleven years old. Terri had spent nearly five years fighting for her life, wanting to be present for her husband and two young boys, but eventually the cancer consumed her body, and she left forever far too soon. Brae and I sat together on the worn out couch of our beach house in Santorini talking late into the night about how this loss had affected him throughout his childhood, adolescence, and now into adulthood, often wondering what it would have been like if she'd been present for the ups and downs of life—how things might have been different, and how he treasured the memories and moments he carried with him. As Brae shared his story with me, his personal fears and frustrations resonated deep inside of me, as these were all worries I had for my own children after losing their dad.

"Happy Birthday dear Addy, Happy Birthday to you," I sang to my sleepy daughter as we woke up in our rented beach house the morning of July 31. "I can't believe you're a year old, my angel. An entire year—and what a year it's been. But you know what? We've made it. You and me. We're in this together. I love you, sweetheart." I whispered to my girl, as she took the opportunity to snuggle her bleached blonde hair into the crook of my neck.

Brae met up with us the night before and the kids were happy to have someone new to shower them with attention, which was made even more apparent as the sounds of Hudson excitedly shouting, "Brae! Brae! Are you awake, Brae!?" down the hallway, signaling the kids were awake and ready to play. I scooped Addy up and walked down the hallway to see if I could rescue Brae from having to wake up yet, but I was too late. Hudson was jumping on the back of the couch, as a still body—in the shape of twenty-three-year-old Brae—was doing his best to hide from view under the very blankets Hudson was jumping on. "Play with me, Brae!"

"Boo!" Brae shouted as he peeled the blankets back, surprising Hudson, who squealed in delight.

And with that, we were all awake. It was still early, but the sun was streaming in the living room and we were all excited about the day ahead. Adeline turned one year old, we were on an insanely beautiful Greek island, and I'd planned for a catamaran cruise down the Santorini coastline. Adeline's first birthday was a significant milestone in this journey of grief—thinking back to where I'd been just one year prior—and I needed to be out on the water, to feel connected to the ocean, to really sort through the overwhelming emotion.

We boarded the beautiful boat, went through our security briefing and were soon underway. The blue ocean to our left, the white, then red, now black sand beaches, made famous by this part of the world, to our right. The sun shone, the children were happy, Kasey and Kayla were enjoying themselves and working on their tans, and Brae captured all of it on film. I smiled. I couldn't remember a time I'd felt prouder of myself than this moment.

"Kasey, Kayla," I said, getting closer to them so that nobody else would hear what I was about to ask her. "Would you please keep the kids busy for a few minutes; I want to spread some of Brian's ashes."

They nodded and I walked toward the bow of the catamaran, where I sat quietly for a few minutes, lost in my own thoughts and memories. *We talked about coming here, babe. Of diving the world together, of what we'd see in Greece. I wish you were here. I miss you so much. The kids miss you. This still doesn't feel real, babe.* The tears started flowing. *Addy turned one today and you never even got to meet her. I want you to know I talk about you all the time. We look at pictures, I tell them all of our crazy stories, and they laugh. I miss you so much, Brian. I really, really miss you.* I grabbed a seashell from his bag of ashes, tears streaming down my face as I filled it with his remains, took a deep breath, and looked out at the horizon as I blew outward, watching his ashes cascade over the side of the boat before getting swept up in the wind and carried away, finding their final resting place on the edge of the deep blue water where he'd stay—his first and only time ever getting to experience these beautiful Greek waters.

I sat on the edge of the catamaran, speaking to Brian and savoring the experience of being here, until a familiar song suddenly belted from the boat's sound system. *There's no way.* I listened intently to determine if I was imagining it, or if this song was truly playing, and then I heard the lyrics of *Live a Life You Will Remember.*

"Mommy, it's the Stay Gold's song!" I could hear Izzy yelling from the back of the boat, the excitement at recognizing the song apparent in her voice.

"It is, sweetheart," I was barely able to say, the tears now flooding my eyes, as I made my way where the kids were all sitting on the net perched above the blue and white waves of the ocean.

I looked from Kasey to Kayla to Brae, who each understood the significance of this song to our family, and who each now had tears in their eyes as well. *This can't be.* I thought, as the song lyrics flooded my memory with images of Brian sailing our 36' sailboat, Stay Gold, from Gig Harbor, Washington, to Honolulu, Hawaii, in the summer of 2017. The lyrics spoke about a father and son. The father advised the son to not take life for granted, to make every moment count, and to enjoy life before it's gone. The song mirrored Brian's life credo as he fully embraced living a life worth remembering, pronounced even more so as he sailed our boat across the Pacific Ocean. In what could only be described as a right-place, right-time scenario, I'd hired Brae to make a film documenting this crazy sailing adventure of Brian's, and Brae had used this song as the main theme song throughout that documentary style film. It was a song synonymous not only with Brian, but the way he lived his life, the way we were attempting to live our lives as well, so it quickly became the "Stay Gold" song and to us it was impossible to hear without thinking of Brian. *I can't believe this song just came on. I can't believe Brae is here with us. I can't believe Izzy remembers this is the Stay Gold song. I can't believe Addy turns one today. I can't believe we're here and he's not.*

"Ash, you OK?" Kasey's question brought me back to reality. *They are all looking at me.*

I looked at Kasey and nodded, smiling as the tears still made their presence known on my cheeks, but slowly transforming from tears of sadness, to tears of pride and of gratitude. These tears were filled with memories of a time when I thought I would no longer see the light of day; of times when I no longer wanted to wake up and face another day without Brian; of times when I thought perhaps life was all over for me. And these tears were filled with the pain I felt, both physically and emotionally, when I was giving birth to Adeline a year ago—the first time I had given birth to one of our children without Brian holding my hand, without him telling me what a great job I was doing, and without him marveling at the sight of our newborn. And now these tears were filled with hope, hope for the future, for countless more smiles, for adventures to remember, and so much more life to live. Brian and I had always talked about the way we wanted to live as a family...adventurous, free, and with no regrets. And there we were, on a catamaran, off the coast of Santorini with my three beautiful children and my incredible friends on the trip of a lifetime: adventurous, free, and living a life with no regrets. *I did it.*

"Happy birthday, Adeline Makai," I whispered to my baby girl, as I held her tight. "You've saved me in more ways than you'll ever realize."

Chapter Sixteen

"What if we don't go back to Athens?" I asked my travel companions as we gathered in the living room to celebrate the final few hours of our time in Santorini.

"What do you mean?" Kasey asked, not sure where I was going with this question.

We had plane tickets purchased, an apartment rented, and a car reserved to take us back to Athens the following morning, where we had planned to spend a few more days before continuing on to our next itinerary stop, but something inside of me was saying, *No-Bucket-List, Ash—live a life you will remember*, and I didn't really want to go back to Athens.

"I don't know..." I started thinking out loud. "We've just had the most incredible time here in Santorini, and we kind of already know what to expect of Athens...I don't really want to go back, do you guys?" I asked, leaving it open to them to help me decide what to do.

"Would we just stay here?" Kasey asked, slightly uncomfortable with the sudden change of plans.

In typical form, I hadn't thought all of the potential questions yet, and at this point I was only throwing the idea out there. We had a car scheduled to pick us up in twelve hours to take us to the airport to catch our flight back to Athens, so I needed to think through this quickly if I was going to pull it off.

"Hmm...we're already over here, we might as well explore another country and take advantage of it. It would cost more to fly all the way here from the United States than to just change plans now and enjoy our time. Is there anywhere you guys want to go? What if we popped over to Paris? Morocco? Malta?" I thought out loud.

"Where's Malta?" Kayla asked.

Sitting on the living room couch, sunburned and still in our bathing suits after spending the day at the beach, I grabbed my computer and typed in the Google search: Malta.

"Oh wow! No way! It's beautiful!" I heard from Kasey, Kayla, and Brae, suddenly huddled around me on the couch and peering over my shoulder as images of the ancient fortress popped up onto my computer screen. I scrolled down looking for more photos to show them, really just buying myself time to plan the logistics of getting the seven of us to Malta in the next twelve hours.

"Are you guys into it?" I asked, a smile on my face in anticipation of the excitement that came with doing something spontaneous like this.

"Let's do it!" Brae said, laughing. Brae reminded me so much of a younger—male—version of myself, always up for adventure and in search of things that brought joy to his life. I knew he'd be OK with the change.

"Kay? Kase?" I asked the girls.

"I mean, OK! If we can do it, let's do it. I'm down." I took these words from the girls as my official group approval to proceed with the itinerary change and two hours later, we had flights booked, a car, and a sailboat Airbnb chartered for our first night on the island.

Next stop, Malta!

"This is insane!" The words kept coming out of each of our mouths as our taxi driver navigated us down distressed one-way streets, zipping in and out of oncoming traffic, as eventually the sandstone-colored fortress in the capital city of Valetta came into view.

"Wow..." It was all any of us could say. We'd never seen anything like it. Because of its geographic location and vast settlement history, Malta is an interesting combination of cultures, with influences from Sicily, North Africa, and Britain, and its surroundings and inhabitants are unlike any other place I've visited before—and it's all surrounded by the bluest-green waters of the Mediterranean Sea. *Stunning.* We pulled into the boat marina, unloaded all of our gear and were soon settled into the fifty-four-foot Beneteau sailboat we'd be calling home for the next twenty-four hours.

Once we'd had a chance to meet the captain, explain who we were, and why we were suddenly on his boat when only twelve hours earlier we'd been planning on spending the day in Athens, we were pulling lines, pouring drinks, and setting sail up the coastline. We spent the next ten hours sailing, swimming, paddle boarding, and creating the most incredible memories together. These were the days I could feel my confidence returning, I knew what I was doing was right, living and enjoying life to the fullest extent with my children at the center of it all. We all celebrated as Izzy jumped off the side of the sailboat into the crystal-clear water below, we laughed as Kayla paddled Adeline and me around the lagoon on the not-quite-big-enough-for-the-three-of-us paddle board and rolled our eyes as Hudson and Brae bonded over making fart noises with their elbows—but still happy to watch them get some boy-time together. These were once-in-a-lifetime memories, and I was grateful to have Brae with us to capture some of them on film.

Eventually the sun began to set and with the sails raised, the sky changing from blue to red to orange behind us as we made our way back toward the marina where we'd spend the night on the sailboat. With the boat safely docked, we ventured out for dinner and ended up gorging ourselves on Maltese style tacos consisting of beans and veggies smothered in a spicy Mediter-ranean green sauce, with sides of tortilla chips and spicy salsa while watching the fireworks explode over the Valetta fortress. It was the perfect end to a perfect day.

"Our car is here, guys!" I announced the next morning as we took one final look at Ace, the sailboat we'd called home the night before, and began our hike up the pier. We'd booked this trip so last-minute that the options for home rentals—which would accommodate seven people—were slightly limited, but I had found a rather bougie villa—think white marble everything, swimming-pool-sized indoor hot tub and sauna, and entire wall of glass doors leading out to the outdoor infinity pool that over-looked the ocean below—all built into a cliffside. We walked in the door, and our jaws dropped. None of us had ever been in—let alone stayed in—anything as extravagant as this before. To be fair, I had found it on a discount travel website and would never have spent the money on it unless it was proceeded with the words; "DISCOUNT" but even that being said, it was a beautiful home and we were going to make it our own for the next few days.

"YOLO!" Kasey broke the silent trance we were all in.

"Mama, what's YOLO?" Izzy looked up at me and asked, squeezing my hand.

"You only live once." I laughed, more at Kasey's use of it, than the term itself. *You only live once is right.* That's why I was at peace with spending the money to make these memories possible for the kids and me, and if those memories were being made in this insanely beautiful home in Malta for the next few days, so be it.

We spent the rest of the day swimming in the pool, deciding who would be hiking up the hill to buy groceries (Kasey and Kayla were the chosen winners) and settling into our Maltese home away from home. When the girls returned, Kasey set to work on barbequing some veggie burgers while Izzy, Hudson, and Brae practiced their jumps and backflips into the pool. *Malta was a good choice.*

"What are we going to do for your birthday, Ash?" Kase asked later that night as we sat on the deck, our skin still warm from the sun we were watching set over the horizon below us.

"Oh, my birthday!" I laughed, more to myself than anyone else. In the back of my mind, I'd known I'd be celebrating my thirty-sixth birthday while in Malta, but I'd been trying my best to not think about it much, because this birthday would be the second birthday I'd celebrate since losing Brian, but the first birthday where I'd be older than he'd lived to be. How could this be? As the kids and my friends started throwing out ideas of how to celebrate my birthday, my thoughts began to wander to my birthday the year before. I'd just given birth to Adeline five days prior, and I still wasn't convinced I'd get myself to a place where I'd live to see thirty-six. Celebrating this birthday was going to be a milestone for me, a huge accomplishment for many reasons, but the first being that I'd made it. I had been able to pull through that deep abyss I had been sinking into and now I was planning to spend my birthday in one of the most exotic and beautiful locations on the planet and there was only one way I wanted to celebrate. "I want to be out on the water. Let's go sailing!" I smiled, looking up at Izzy, Hudson, and Adeline, who clapped their hands and exchanged excited squeals of laughter.

The morning of August 4, we woke up, grabbed the kids' life jackets, a bit of sunscreen and were on our way to another marina, this time on the island of Goza—one of the other islands of the Republic of Malta. We were greeted by Paul, a tanned, fit sailboat skipper who was quick to ask where our husbands were, and equally quick to offer to get the boat bar opened early when we explained why we were on this trip—and the fact it was my birthday—and there was no place any of us would rather be than all together, with Paul now, in Malta and on his sailboat for the day. Paul was an incredible host, pointing to a map of where we were, where we'd be sailing, and places we could stop along the way to swim. With the safety briefing done, the sails were hoisted, the boat bar was opened, and we were officially underway. *Maybe thirty-six isn't so bad after all.*

We spent the next few hours sailing into the wind, stopping to drop anchor and explore little caverns and rock formations from the water below. Izzy, Hudson, and Addy each took turns jumping into the comfortably warm water, laughing and splashing about as we pointed to fish—and eventually a few jellyfish—before returning to the safety of the swim ladder where we climbed aboard, wrapped up in our towels, and raised the anchor to sail toward our next destination. The ocean, my children, a sailboat, adventure, laughter, travel; these were some of the best moments of my post-Brian life so far, and I was soaking them up.

"Oh man, jet skis! Those look like so much fun!" I said excitedly to Kasey sitting next to me. We had just dropped anchor near a lagoon and there were a handful of small boats and jet skis buzzing all around us. "Hey Paul! Can people rent those jet skis?" I didn't want to get my hopes up.

"Oh yeah! My buddy has a few, I'll give him a call." He winked, happy to play his part in making this day even more special for us.

Twenty minutes later, I was gripping the handlebars of a black-and-blue-striped jet ski. Kasey sat behind me with her arms wrapped around my waist and we jet skied at full power through the open Mediterranean Sea. I'd never been on a jet ski before, and with every wave we hit, we nearly flew off the seats as the ski bouncing up and down through the white-capped waves. I couldn't help but laugh. The waves splashed up, wind whipped through our hair, salt-water sprayed across my face, and I savored this moment of time. *What a day. What a life! This is amazing.*

We eventually made our way back to the boat only to find the winds had picked up a bit while we'd been playing around. Paul told us to get comfy and that we'd take a few hours to get back to port, so we grabbed some snacks and settled in for the long ride home. The winds really picked up and the kids were feeling a little seasick, so we held them in our laps and they dozed in and out of sleep as we chatted with Paul.

"I have to admit I'm surprised you'd bring such young kids out on a boat." Paul admitted at one point.

"These kids have probably been on a sailboat more than most adults you know!" Kasey immediately got defensive, thinking he was questioning my judgement in bringing Izzy, Hudson, and Adeline out with us—especially since we were now facing some rough waters and the comfort level had slowly depleted. We'd heard the criticism and skepticism from people near and far over the past seven weeks, and Kasey was protective of me and the kids. This moment was no exception. It certainly wasn't the first—nor the last—comment of its kind from locals who couldn't understand why on Earth would I embark on such a demanding journey with three children under the age of six. Truth be told, even some of my relatives and friends back home had tried to persuade me from traveling through seven—well, now eight—countries in Europe with children who were so little and wouldn't remember much, if anything, of the trip anyway. I tried countless times to explain to them that what mattered to me wasn't that they'd remember, but that we were making memories together as a family now. I was raising them to not be afraid of taking chances if you see the value in them, to live a life of adventure, family, and love. Because that's who we are as a family. Paul didn't mean any harm by his comment, I'm positive our group wasn't his typical guest, and in reality, it was a compliment to know that despite it not being "normal," we were still doing it, still here, and still living our best lives. We spent the next few hours sharing stories of sailing adventures, family, loss, and travel. By the time we pulled into the marina, the sun had set, the kids were all sound asleep, and Paul hugged me goodbye as he asked to stay in touch. He said we'd made him a believer in what we were doing.

Malta had been a turning point for us in the trip, we couldn't articulate it, but could each feel it. The sunshine, the ocean, the laughter, the adventure, taking each day and just enjoying it as a group. These were the moments we'd each craved and that were made so prevalent in this country. This was it. We drove home to our rented villa to spend one last night on the deck and to share stories and favorite moments of our time there. Brae filmed as everyone sang *Happy Birthday* to me, and the kids surprised me with a homemade lemon cake they'd baked—with the help of Kasey and Kayla—the night before. It had been a happy birthday indeed and I felt full of gratitude—of what had been, of what was in the moment, and all that was ahead—I was ready for it. We'd be leaving Malta in the morning, and just like leaving thirty-five for thirty-six, I was sad to say goodbye, but excited for what was ahead.

Chapter Seventeen

"Hudson, where are we!?" I asked as we stepped off the airplane and into the crisp, cool, Irish air. "We're in Ireland!" Hudson exclaimed, wrapping his arms tightly around my neck.

"Say it again, bud! Where are we!?" I smiled as I pulled him in tighter and kissed his chubby cheek. Brae stood a few feet behind with his video camera trained on us to capture the moment.

"We're in Ireland, Mama!" He laughed. "Brrr...it's cold here!"

It was 2011 when I first stepped foot in Ireland during a backpacking trip across the United Kingdom with my little brother, Benny. I had scoured the Google Flights app looking for the cheapest plane tickets to get us to Europe and when I saw these pop up, I called Benny and said, "let's go!" We saved every single penny we'd made for six months to be able to afford this trip, staying in twelve-dollar-a-night hostels in rooms shared with eleven other people, eating food sold exclusively by street vendors because it was the most affordable, learning bus and train schedules because we didn't have enough money to rent a car, and yet I also vividly remember taking the airport shuttle through the countryside toward downtown Dublin and watching, completely mesmerized, as flickers of the green and gold landscape flashed by our window. The air was so clean and fresh, it had the familiar scent of home back in the Pacific Northwest, but there was something special here, something I couldn't put my finger on, but that I immediately felt drawn to. Our shuttle bus had taken a sharp turn at the crest of a hill, and I turned my head to the right and there she was: the mighty Irish coast. The coast was the deepest bluish-green hue I'd ever seen, the white caps splashing across the surface, only illuminating these intense colors of nature. It was love at first sight for me. I'd been in the country for only twenty minutes, but I immediately felt at home. Benny and I spent the next few days exploring Ireland's east coast, having drinks with people from around the world at Temple Bar Pub, watching an Irish dance performance, eating vegetarian versions of bangers and mash, and exploring a number of charming coastal towns via the local metro train.

It had been seven years since I'd last been here, but needless to say, stepping foot on this beautiful land again, with all three of my children in tow, was nostalgic for me, and I was ecstatic to be back.

"Can you guys believe we're here?" I asked.

In actuality, this leg of the trip held special meaning to each of us and was one of the places we were all most looking forward to visiting. Kayla was excited to come here because her brother had been fascinated with Ireland for as long as she could remember, and she was excited to experience it on his behalf and call home to tell him about it. For Kasey, traveling to Ireland was a way to honor her little brother's memory, and one she'd hoped to do long before this trip was even a possibility. Johnny had passed away when he was just seventeen years old and his childhood dream was to visit the land of their family heritage, to research their fair-skinned ancestors and to visit MacCurtain Street in Cork—the source of their familial name. This was an important experience for Kasey, and she knew this was where she'd be scattering the ashes of her brother, dad and grandma Nana, in a touching and memorable tribute between her and the land of those who had passed before her.

"I can't believe I'm actually here," Kasey whispered. "Ash, I can't tell you what this means to me to be here and with you all."

We drove from the Dublin airport across the Irish countryside in search of Chapelbride Manor, the lodge I'd rented as our home for the next ten days. We drove past farms and fields of wild yellow Furze, we crossed diverse landscapes and through small towns, and I looked out the window in front of me and recognized the same green and gold colors I'd experienced in 2011, the ones I'd come to know as what I regarded as the essence of Ireland. The feeling was back, and I was excited to share it with Isabel, Hudson, Adeline, and my friends currently piled in the car with me.

"Mama, I'm tired," Hudson called from the backseat. We'd been driving for over an hour and the kids were starting to fidget.

"Ugh, are we there yet? I'm hungryyyy," Izzy whined.

"I know kiddo, we're almost there!" I lied, looking at Kasey in my rearview mirror for support in helping to distract the kids.

She caught my look and smiled, then leaned forward, and whispered, "Hey Ash, if you see a spot to pull over—I kind of have to go to the bathroom."

Ha! The joys of travel. Are we there yet?

It took us a few loops and laps on unmarked country roads, and eventually a call to our gracious host as the afternoon turned to evening and our GPS still couldn't locate the Manor, but eventually, we found our way, pulled in the gravel driveway, and were greeted with the sight of a home you'd expect to find in the Irish countryside. The Manor was a two-story, white stone, box-shaped lodge with a brick pathway leading to the arched doorway, keeping the hundred-year-old antiques inside safe from the farm animals roaming freely all around us.

"This is siiick!" I heard Brae say, leaning forward from his seat next to me to take it all in. This truly was an incredible sight—quite the change of scenery from the heat and sandstone colors we'd just experienced in Malta—but with the emerald-green trees and open field across the road, the crumbling stone wall separating us from the cows and sheep walking toward us assuming it was dinner time—this was what you'd expect from Ireland, and we were excited and thankful for it. The kids were beyond ready for bed after a long day of traveling and we all walked through the home claiming a bedroom before dropping our stuff.

"Alright, what do you guys want to do tomorrow?" I asked once we'd dined on the potato chips and half-frozen pizza we'd bought at the gas station during the drive in. "Tomorrow is Brae's last day with us before he has to fly home, so we should drive into the city and explore Dublin, if that sounds fun to you guys?"

"That sounds good!" Kasey responded, always game for anything and happy to finally be there.

"Can we go to the Guinness factory? I told my brother I'd bring home something from there for him." Kayla asked.

"Sure! Let's drive into the city and then we can either walk or take a bus around, see where the day takes us." This was how I liked to travel, making up plans as we went along, depending on the situation and how we were all feeling.

We woke up early the next morning, energized and excited to explore a new city. We backtracked our way into the city center. When Benny and I visited in 2011, we hadn't rented a car, but I knew there was parking near the Dublin Zoo and from there we could catch a hop-on, hop-off bus to take us around town so that I wouldn't have to drive to each of the destinations we wanted to explore. After a few more unexpected loops and laps through the Irish countryside—we'll call it an unplanned sightseeing tour—we eventually arrived at the Dublin Zoo and found a parking spot on the street. Brae pulled out his video camera and filmed us walking down the sidewalk in front of him, the kids pointing excitedly as the multicolored sightseeing busses whizzed past us.

"I want to go on the red bus, Brae!" Hudson exclaimed into the camera, in a voice only a three-year-old boy could achieve as he realized he was about to get on a giant bus for a day full of adventure with his best friends.

"Alright bud, let's do it!" Brae smiled back.

Brae and Hudson had formed a special bond these past few weeks, the two boys banding together among a group of women and taking moments such as these to revel in the same type of excitement.

***

"I'm sad for my own kids who will have to go through all of this too." I admitted to him. "Especially Hudson, who won't even remember his dad in a few years. He won't even know how much Brian loved him. How funny his dad was. Every little boy needs their dad to look up to, and he won't get that." The gravity of this realization hitting me as I shared my fears with Brae. Tears were suddenly in my eyes, stinging my cheeks as they made their way down my face.

"Brian was such a cool guy. I feel so lucky to have met him and worked with him a little bit, and that because of him, I now get to be a part of this with all of you guys. But I know you're a really cool mom, too, and you're showing Izzy, Hudson, and Addy what's important in life. There aren't a lot of moms out there who'd take their kids on a trip like this. You're doing it right, Ash." Brae offered this gift to me, the voice of reason from a child who lost a parent, to a parent who'd been raising children in the same position, and it was the reassurance I needed in the moment.

"You and my mom would have gotten along really well." Brae confided in me. "She was really smart and incredibly strong. She was a fighter, just like you. She was a really great writer and kept this blog online about her experience through everything. She actually wrote me a letter, too, which I found after she passed away," he continued.

Brae's mom, Terri gave him the gift of her words and motherly advice:

Dear Brae,

Just remember that when you are faced with a tough decision, listen to your heart. The answer is there. Don't get caught up in what everyone else is doing. Be your own self, genuine and authentic. Be You.

I love you,
Mom

These words, written by a woman I never had the opportunity to meet, but whose son was sitting next to me as he read them—half a world away from where they were originally written—struck me to the core. Brian lived these words; these were the values and legacy he left for his three young children, and to see Brae, who had experienced a fate similar to my own children, but whose mom gifted him these words, and through his own actions was now living up to them, was a truly special realization.

Brae was an incredibly well-rounded, adventurous, fun-loving, special human being, and regardless of the circumstances that life threw at him as a child, he grew into a man his mom would have been so incredibly proud of. Brae gave me hope that my own children, despite the sad circumstances bestowed upon them at such a young age, would go on to do great things too. I felt very fortunate to understand we were all in this together, and Izzy, Hudson, and Adeline were so lucky to be surrounded by so many incredible people, with such varied life experiences that would help them carry and navigate whatever the future holds.

***

With Hudson's prompting, we caught the red sightseeing bus that took us past the centuries-old churches and cathedrals and dropped us of in front of the Ha'penny Bridge, a Dublin institution famous for once charging its patrons ha' penny (half a penny) for using it to cross the river running through downtown.

We treated ourselves to an Irish breakfast of espresso, eggs, and oatmeal at a local café before stepping back out onto the crowded sidewalks lining downtown Dublin and began walking with no real destination in mind, just anxious to soak up the excitement happening all around us. We walked into a few shops, bought souvenirs, crossed back and forth over the River Liffey, and soon arrived at the iconic brick red building I'd come to know as Temple Bar Pub on my previous visit to Dublin.

"You guys! We have to go in here." I looked at my traveling companions. With four adults and three small children—one in a bright pink stroller—we were not an inconspicuous group of people. How could we pull this off?

"What if we take turns?" Kayla offered. "I'll stay with the kids while you guys go have a drink, and then we can switch when you're done."

"Yes! Let's do it!" I was excited. I knew that just inside those walls, there was an Irish man with a guitar in his hand currently serenading the crowd with songs that would have everyone signing along—not to mention a wall full of various brands of gin, a few of which were about to have my name on them. We made our plan and soon after Kasey, Brae, and I were seated at a high-top table up front, the red-neon "Temple Bar" sign illuminating the small wooden stage below.

Time went by quickly there—and so did the drinks. We chatted, we laughed, we drank, and we listened to Irish men playing guitars and singing. I felt so alive and relaxed—and "glowy" as my Irish Catholic grandma used to say after enjoying a few glasses of wine. Brae and I held our own, keeping up with each other as Kasey and Kayla took turns having a drink and then heading back outside to take the kids to lunch and for a bit more exploring. It was a perfect afternoon of laughter, friendship, and just living in the moment, but eventually it was time to sip the last remaining drops of drinks, sing the last few lyrics of the cover songs, and head home.

"I'll miss you!" Hudson cried sweetly as he hugged Brae's neck the following morning. We were back at the Dublin airport, dropping Brae off for his flight home, and Hudson wasn't happy that his new-found best friend and the only other dude on this trip with us was having to say goodbye for now.

"I'm going to miss you, too, Bud! But we'll hang out when you guys get home, OK?" Brae hugged him back.

Separated by twenty years of age but sharing the same youthful exuberance for life, Hudson and Brae had formed a special brotherly bond and it was hard to watch the two of them part. For all of us, Brae's departure meant our trip was officially winding down, and we'd all be headed home soon. We waved our final goodbyes and drove in silence for a while, each considering what this trip meant for us and how it had changed us. We were all somewhat lost in thought when eventually the coastal town of Greystones came into view and we decided to spend the day there exploring, our spirits suddenly renewed at the scent of fresh air and sight of the ocean in front of us. I visited this town with my brother, and I remember falling in love with it as soon as I stepped off the train. Its main street filled with small boutiques, cafes, and coffee shops extending warm invites as we made our way toward the beach entrance. After a long drive, the kids were excited to stretch their legs and have an excuse to play in the sand, so we grabbed a snack and walked past the shops toward the beach.

"Hey Kay, could you take a photo of me scattering some of Brian's ashes here?" I asked Kayla, while Kasey, Izzy, Hudson, and Addy all busied themselves with burying each other in the sand.

"Sure! I can totally see Brian loving it here," Kayla said gently as she took a few photos of me spreading my love into the deep teal ocean in front of me.

"He really would. We talked about moving here someday, and I actually have it in my will that I'd like the kids to scatter some of my ashes here too after I die. Hopefully a long, long, long time from now, but I think it would be pretty amazing to be reunited with him here like this." I responded, thinking about my kids standing in this same spot, much later in life, knowing their mom and dad would be reunited in a place they stood as young children with me.

After taking a walk by the ocean, we visited a few jewelry shops and looked for the perfect piece of jewelry that would remind us of our visit to Ireland. I found myself a single silver bangle to adorn my right wrist, while Kasey found a Claddagh ring and Kayla marveled at the diamond rings, taking note for a future boyfriend to potentially propose with some day. The day went by slowly, in a relaxing manner, filled with genuine smiles and lots of great memories.

"Tell Rory I sent you," read part of the message my friend David from back home sent me. David and I had connected through the technical diving community shortly after Brian's death and as a lifelong explorer and rebreather diver himself, he had been instrumental in helping me navigate the intricacies of understanding how exactly my husband died. He knew I would be visiting Ireland, and wanted me to meet with his friend Rory, a sixty-ish-year-old man who David had met while on an expedition to explore the *Titanic*. I texted Rory, knowing nothing else about him other than the address of the scuba diving shop he owned outside of Greystones, and that my friend David said he was alright.

"Come on in!" Rory texted me back, and we turned the car in his direction.

"I never met your husband," he said once we'd arrived, met, hugged, and introduced everyone, "but I've shared his story with all the people I know."

The technical scuba diving community is incredibly small, and Brian's story had been shared widely amongst the adventurers and explorers of the group, so while Rory and I had led completely separate lives up until that point, the fact he had read about Brian's accident and was taking the time to connect with me and the kids was truly special.

"I have a boat if you'd all like to go out for a bit," he offered. "The waters are usually choppy though, so I don't know if the wee ones would be up for it."

"Ahh these kids are troopers." I smiled. "They've grown up on boats, I think they'll be alright." I said as I happily accepted his invite.

A few days later, we all met back up with Rory and piled into his inflatable dive boat—donning life jackets, sweatshirts, and foul weather gear—and set off for an afternoon of exploring the Irish Coast via Dublin Bay—before making our way out to the open ocean. Our new friend expertly maneuvered his boat through the waves and wakes of the feisty sea, pointing to long-abandoned castles on the land to our right, and some of the local sea life in the water to our left. This was not your typical sightseeing trip of Dublin and we were all thrilled for the unique opportunity.

"Would you like to see something really special?" Rory asked Izzy, Hudson, and Adeline, who suddenly looked as if they belonged in a storybook. Three young children living their wildest dreams: sailing the high seas in a foreign port, with an old captain full of remarkable tales of adventure and expedition. It couldn't get better than that until we suddenly crossed a small channel and Rory maneuvered his boat up to a concrete block attached to an island.

"Here we are, right? Have you kids ever been on a deserted island before?" Rory laughed with his thick Irish accent, his voice matching the excitement in his own eyes. An adventurer to his core, Rory was still a kid at heart, and getting to pass on moments like these to children, the next generation of explorers, was something I could tell delighted him to no end.

"Ashley," Kayla said, "I cannot believe that we just met this man, and now we're here with him on a deserted island in the middle of the ocean." Her words told me she was outside of her comfort zone, but this was a journey of pushing ourselves and of embracing opportunities, and that's exactly what we were doing in that moment.

"I know. It's incredible, right?" I beamed. These were the moments and experiences that made me feel alive, that made me appreciate the time we had here. I smiled as I watched Izzy and Hudson hike up the hill ahead of me, Kasey carrying Addy, Kayla behind them, each pushing themselves physically and emotionally to make it to the top. The kids and I were on a similar climb in our journey through grief, working together to push each other when needed, but understanding we had to do to the work to get there, and it would take time. This trip would soon be coming to an end, but the lessons learned, and the connections created would carry us forward for the rest of our lives. *I'm sure of it.* We were the only people on Dalkey Island that day. We hiked to the top, took in 360-degree views of the ocean crashing around us, laughed as Izzy and Hudson raced each other through the rubble of the ancient buildings, and took countless photos in an attempt to capture the essence of these memories. As we made our way back to shore, I looked at my children—now tired and doing their best to stay awake—and smiled. This trip had been everything I had hoped for and more.

"So where are you headed next?" Rory asked before waving goodbye to us.

"Iceland!" Izzy yelled. "Back to Iceland."

Chapter Eighteen

I'm not ready for this to be over yet. With every airplane, train, and car we took, each street corner we passed and every road we traveled, I felt my confidence gaining momentum and returning to my soul. It was nearly tangible by the time we touched down in Iceland. We had two nights to spend in the land of fire and ice, before boarding the plane that would take us "home." If these two months had taught be anything, however, it was that home wasn't defined by four walls; it wasn't our cozy beds and comfortable blankets; it wasn't the clothes in our closet; or the cars in the driveway; it wasn't the treasures we'd collected over the years from our travels; or even the photos hanging on the light gray walls of our living room. Instead, these past two months had truly proven what the cheesy wooden sign that hung by the door of my childhood home had read: Home is Where Your Heart is.

"We're here, you guys! I'm so freaking happy, but so sad at the same time. I can't believe this is it." It was hard to suppress all of the memories and emotion that touching down in Iceland had brought up for me.

As a family and a group of travelers, we'd experienced our share of dicey moments throughout these travels, from strategic setbacks—losing the luggage in Amsterdam, booking the Airbnb on the wrong day, running out of water in Athens, stressing over a melted birthday cake in Switzerland—to emotional breakdowns, such as coming to terms with the reality of the magnitude of absolutely senseless loss at the Auschwitz concentration camp, feeling overwhelmed at the Matterhorn, celebrating Adeline's first birthday; reflecting on the reality that it was a full year since giving birth to her, and realizing that things could have looked very different had I not chosen to fight through my sadness. But we'd also experienced the most incredible moments together, from getting on the first airplane that took us from New York City to Amsterdam with butterflies in my stomach thinking, *I'm actually doing this!* to discovering the beauty of Norway and understanding exactly why Brian loved it so much, to watching the wind sweep through the kids' hair as we sailed through the blue-green waters of Malta. There were so many highlights, incredible moments and, as our plane touched down in Iceland, everything we accomplished just caught up with me.

Iceland, our last stop.

"I can't believe I'm going to see the Blue Lagoon!" Kasey was more than enthused knowing she'd soon be soaking in the mysterious and world-famous milky blue waters of the Blue Lagoon. "This is seriously one of the things I've been most excited about this entire trip."

I strategically built Iceland into our itinerary for a multitude of reasons. First and foremost, it would help break up the travel time home a bit. Izzy, Hudson, and Addy were seasoned travelers, but even they had their limits of sitting still on an airplane before they needed to run around. Shaving even a few hours off a flight from Ireland to Portland, Oregon, by means of stopping in Iceland for a few days was worth it to me, which meant by the time we were ready to head home, we'd be looking at a seven-hour flight from Iceland instead of a ten-hour flight from Ireland. Those little decisions made a world of difference when traveling with small children—especially since I wanted to keep travel a fun and positive experience for them and pushing them too hard on a long flight might have had adverse consequences for future travel. Second, Kasey really wanted to see the Blue Lagoon, and after two months of travel, a few days in Iceland wasn't really out of the way, so why not? Third, and arguably the real reason for this layover of sorts, was that Iceland held a very special place in my heart and being that we were on a journey of healing and making new memories as a family of four, I couldn't fathom flying over this beautiful country on our way home without stopping to reflect on the different seasons of life that had previously brought me to this country.

In 2010, I was sitting behind my desk at work in the bank—in the same swivel chair I'd be sitting in three years later when Brian called me for the first time, the phone call that changed the entire trajectory of my future—and while on break, I stumbled upon a fairly inexpensive plane ticket to Iceland. I knew nothing about the country, except that it was an island in the middle of the ocean, it looked full of adventures waiting to be had, and it would cost me $650 to get there. I was single, had a week of vacation time to use, and a backpack in my closet constantly filled with travel essentials and ready to go.

I booked the ticket without a second thought, and a few months later I touched down in Reykjavik, Iceland, as a single, solo, twenty-six-year-old traveler, out on an adventure. I was immediately awestruck. Black volcanic rock laid tucked beneath layer upon layer of white snow, icy blue waters circled the island and offering the most beautiful juxtaposition to the rugged landscape. Mile upon mile of uninhabited land stretched as far as the eye could see until it suddenly dropped off into the abyss of the Atlantic Ocean. I spent my week there exploring the sights and sounds of downtown Reykjavik, horseback riding through the snow-covered countryside, snorkeling above the Silfra—the North American and Eurasian tectonic plates in Thingvelier National Park—soaking in the milky-blue waters of the geothermal pools at the Blue Lagoon, experiencing the delightfully painful hangover after a night of drinking Icelandic Schnapps—also known as Black Death—and finally visiting *Hallgrimskirkja*, one of the tallest buildings in Iceland. You could enter the building for free and look around, but once inside, for the best experience, you paid a few Icelandic Krona to take the elevator ride to the top. From here you enjoyed panoramic views of downtown Reykjavik, the brightly colored buildings and streets below where, if you squinted just right, you could watch the waves of the ocean lapping at the shore below. It was the most incredible week, in one of the most strangely beautiful places I'd ever seen. I loved it and knew I'd return some day.

The second time I visited the country was in the spring of 2017 with two-year-old Izzy and eight-month-old Hudson in tow. Brian was busy at home getting Stay Gold ready to sail from Washington to Hawaii, and as I wouldn't be joining him on this Transpacific crossing, I was in desperate need of an adventure of my own. I found inexpensive tickets to Scotland, and figured while I was in the area, I might as well introduce the kids to the adventure of visiting Iceland in the wintertime.

"Seriously?" Brian asked in between bites of homemade veggie stir-fry after I shared the news of our upcoming trip with him. While this would not probably be normal dinner conversation for most American families, this was how Brian and I lived our lives together, supporting each other and wanting great things for one another and our children, even if we couldn't participate. "I wish I could go! That sounds freaking awesome. When are you going?" This was what most of our conversations sounded like, one of us coming at the other with a big idea, and the other encouraging it. I knew he'd be supportive.

Brian and I had talked about visiting Iceland together, putting it on our Dive Dream List to dive Silfra, but between having babies, moving, and other travel, we hadn't found the time yet to visit together, so instead I'd bring the kids this time and Brian would join us the next time.

A few weeks later, Brian drove the kids and I to the airport, hugged and kissed us goodbye, and asked me to send lots of photos. Izzy, Hudson, and I spent our time abroad exploring the same streets I had walked seven years earlier, making sure to pay our 1,000 Krona to take the elevator to the top of Hallgrimskirkja and take in those same sights of downtown Reykjavik I had on my last visit. I held Izzy and Hudson in my arms and looked out the barred windows from the top of the building, and I couldn't believe how much my life had changed for the better these past seven years since I last stood in this same spot—I was married to my best friend, a supportive, handsome, passionate, wonderful explorer, we had two beautiful children together, and we were about to move to paradise. What an incredible life I was living.

And now it was 2019, and I was returning to Iceland for the third time, in yet another phase of my life. I looked out the window of our plane as the now familiar landscape came into view. After two months of traveling together, we had our system down to a science, and Kasey, Kayla, and I smiled knowingly at each other as we grabbed our backpacks, car seats, and all three kids—while watching the families around us scrambling and struggling to contain their own overflowing luggage carts and exhausted children.

"Oh man, he's gonna lose that one!" We laughed quietly as we witnessed a weary traveler attempt to tackle the luggage cart he had overfilled, causing it to tip over in the middle of the walkway, losing each and every bag he'd piled onto it. *Whoops!*

We drove the ninety minutes from Keflavik airport across the black volcanic rocks I'd come to know as the iconic telltale sign that I was in Iceland. I guided our car through downtown Reykjavik, trying (and more than once, failing) to remember to stay on the right side of the road as I'd just spent ten days driving on the left side of the road in Ireland—it was not as easy as you'd imagine switching back!

"This is crazy!" I needed a second set of eyes on the road with me, especially while turning onto new streets from stop signs. "Tell me if I switch into the wrong lane, okay?"

We drove, and drove, and drove, making it outside of the city somehow unscathed, and eventually came across a beautiful lake surrounded by trees, which led us to a gravel road, and then a tree-lined path and a gate with a lockbox on it. I typed in the code, waited for it to click, and anxiously pulled it open to reveal what was awaiting us on the other side: an Icelandic cabin in the woods: our home for the next few days.

"Welcome!" We'd made it, our last home, on the last stop, of our last country of this adventure.

We unpacked what we needed from the car, rationalizing that we'd only be here for two nights and didn't need *everything*—but really just not wanting to make any more trips than necessary carrying gear up the steep incline of a trail leading from the car to the cabin. It was surprising how little you could be OK with if it saved you from having to carry heavy things and children up a steep hill.

We settled into the two-bedroom cabin for the night, cooking a feast of the Icelandic veggie burgers and frozen fries we'd scored at the grocery store on the way in, and eating nearly an entire package of *Kinder* chocolates before admitting that, even though it was still light out, we were all exhausted from traveling all day.

"Where does everyone want to sleep?" I asked, looking around.

The cabin was small. Two bedrooms for six people, three of which were young kids who flailed their limbs like they were fighting dinosaurs in their sleep.

"Addy can sleep in my room. Kasey and Izzy, are you guys good together? Kay and Hudson on the pull-out bed in the living room? If that sucks, we can switch it up tomorrow," I half-asked, half-announced, exhausted, and ready for bed.

We'd spent many nights in varying accommodations across the continent of Europe these past two months, but next to the sailboat we'd slept on in Malta, this was by far the coziest of accommodations.

"Sounds good. Goodnight!" Everyone was tired, and with such a small space, and our last two nights, there was no real reason to barter with sleeping accommodations.

We slept well that night but woke up early the next morning to a somber feeling in the cabin. We'd be flying home the next day and this incredible experience would be over. Those were big emotions to process in a small cabin and it was hard to hide. Kasey, Kayla, and I filled our coffee cups and toasted to one another, acknowledging it was coming to an end, but how incredible it had all been.

"At least Hudson's knees will have a chance to heal!" Kasey exclaimed, breaking the tension as we laughed, recalling how many times he'd tripped over the uneven pavement in Amsterdam, leaving him with scabs and scars on his knees.

"Oh my gosh, but that cheese dish in Greece! Do you think you can order it online?" Kayla joked. It was the best food we'd eaten the entire trip and we hadn't been able to stop talking about it.

"Ughh. I'm not ready for this to be over you guys. I could keep going." I looked from Kasey to Kayla to Izzy, Hudson, and Addy, understanding what we'd accomplished, but realizing we'd be interpreting the lessons learned from it for months and years to come. "We still have two more days though...it's not over yet!" I was trying to stay positive and enjoy the time we had left.

We finished our coffee, got the kids dressed, and hiked our way back down the hill to the car. Today's adventure would take us to soak in the Blue Lagoon geothermal spa. One of the twenty-five wonders of the world, you could see the steam rising from the milky-blue water through the lava fields for miles before you arrived on site. The water, drawn to the surface through geothermal extraction wells and piping hot by the time it reached this pool-of-sorts, was thought to be full of healing, rejuvenating, and nourishing properties. To me, it was uniquely Iceland, an experience only available in this remote region of the world, and the fact it had a swim up bar where you could order ice-cold beer and cider with a blue-mud face mask on, was a win in my book.

"Oooooh it's warm!" Izzy exclaimed as she dipped her toes in.

We spent the next few hours floating around, dipping Addy's toes into the water and taking turns walking the kids to the bathrooms, snack bar, and for a swim around the lagoon as they relaxed on the surface in their bright orange swim floaties. They looked ridiculous floating on the water's surface in this lavish spa in Iceland, but this was normal to them, the way we lived life, and they didn't notice they were the youngest people present that day.

"Mom, watch this!" Hudson beckoned my attention as he leapt from the wooden bridge above us into my arms, splashing the hot blue water below. The kids were happy, Kasey, Kayla, and I were happy, and this was a perfect last full day before heading home. Our time at the Blue Lagoon was drawing to a close and we had a long drive ahead of us to get back to the cabin, but there was one more place I wanted—needed—to visit before leaving Iceland.

Hallgrimskirkja. Hard to pronounce, but easy to recognize, it zigzagged cement architecture towers over the brightly painted shops and restaurants lining the streets of downtown Reykjavik. I had taken the elevator and climbed the stairs to the very top of this building twice before. It felt like a pilgrimage of sorts, returning to the only place on Earth I'd experienced such defining experiences, at different stages of my life, and I knew this needed to be the final stop of this healing tour for me.

"Hey Kase, can you snap a photo of the kids and me?" I asked, trying to choke back tears, but feeling the emotions flooding through me. I had a photo of Izzy, Hudson, and me standing in this spot two years earlier, and a selfie from nine years ago.

"No problem, Ash." She responded, not necessarily understanding the gravity of the moment for me, but recognizing it was an important one. "Everyone say, cheeeeese!"

Kasey, Kayla, Izzy, Hudson, Addy, and I took our time walking around the viewing platform that afternoon. A small area, no bigger than the average American living room, but with open-air windows you could look out in every direction of the island from, we took photos, pointed to the buildings below, talked about our flight home the next day, and how we'd be traveling across the ocean we were now viewing.

"Hey guys, can you keep an eye on the kids for me for a second?" I asked the girls in the telltale way they'd come to know over the past two months as meaning I needed a few moments to myself.

"We got this, Ash." Kayla responded, lifting Hudson up to look out the window and point to something below.

I'd scattered Brian's ashes in every country we'd visited so far, and I knew with certainty I wanted to keep some for the very end, to scatter from this spot, to preserve this memory in my mind forever. I tucked myself into a corner, looked out at the ocean, talked to myself, to Brian, to the world below and let the tears flow.

Well, babe, this is it. Our final stop, our final country, our final destination. I wish you were here with us. I wish you could see us, see the kids, see me. I wish we were making these memories together. I really hope you know how much we love you. How much we miss you, how we'd give anything to have you back here with us. I know you'd be so proud of me, for taking our kids on this trip. For confronting the hard moments, for pushing past the fear and the sadness, to live life. I promise I'll keep taking the kids on adventures. I promise I'll raise them how we wanted to, that I'll show them the world, and that we'll continue to travel. I just wish you were here with us. I miss you, Brian. I really really miss you.

This had been an incredible journey, in more ways than I'd given myself the credit, time, or emotional capacity to think through, but there I was, there we were, and we'd made it. I wiped my eyes, feeling proud of myself, proud of my kids, proud of my family and what we'd accomplished, and I stepped back from the window.

"All right, you guys ready to go home?" I asked with a smile across my face.

"To the cabin, or home, home?" Izzy asked.

"Yes." I responded with a smile. My girl was so smart, so intuitive, so aware.

I'd found my confidence again. I wasn't the same woman who had stood in this exact spot previously. I would never be the person again, but in this moment, I knew with certainty that I could do this. I could raise these three kids, I could be a great mom, I could be an explorer, an adventurer, a traveler. I could honor Brian and all that he brought to my life, and the beautiful family he helped me create, and I could share that with our children, and with everyone else out there willing to listen. In this moment, I knew I had made it. The kids and I had made it.

Our time in Iceland was coming to an end, but our new dynamic as a family of four was just beginning. We had conquered what we'd set out to do, we'd traveled across Europe, we'd made new memories, we'd regained our confidence. Three adults, three kids, three backpacks, three car seats. Eight countries, two months. We'd laughed, we'd cried, we'd explored, we'd gotten lost, and we'd celebrated. The lessons learned during these two months could fill volumes of books, and still not adequately describe or explain how important this journey was for us both individually and as a family.

The next morning, we packed our bags, hauled them back down the hill to the car, guided our last rental car of the trip through Reykjavik to board our last flight of this journey. With expert precision we loaded and unloaded our gear, got checked in, passed through security, boarded our flight, settled the kids down, and soon everyone was asleep. Seven hours later we arrived at the Portland International Airport, tired and emotional, but alive and well. One by one we watched our bags come out of the conveyer belt, followed by the car seats—Izzy's, then Hudson's, then...

"Do you guys see Addy's car seat anywhere?" I asked.

"Hmm...nope." Kasey and Kayla responded in unison.

"Wouldn't that be funny if after all these countries, and all these flights, without anything lost, it was the final leg home where the baby's car seat is lost? And in our own home airport?" I laughed out loud at the irony, not really believing that could happen...

Except, it happened.

Welcome Home!

Conclusion

Two years have passed since we returned home from that trip. Three years have passed since I last kissed Brian's lips and since the kids last heard their dad's voice. Time has a way of playing tricks on us, especially as we grow older and memories start to fade and blur, as we become consumed with our daily lives, family, work, responsibilities... we're always planning and preparing for the future and what's ahead. Reading through these stories I've shared with you, remembering page upon page of my own personal heartache and the deepest, darkest moments of my entire life dispersed between some of the most life changing and pride-filled ones to see how far I've come in such a short period of time is a journey all in its own for me. Even as I read these words, these chapters of my life, it's hard to believe this really is my story. To those of you all reading this book, these are stories of love and loss, sadness, despair, travel, and adventure, of a family you don't know who has lived through something extraordinary. To me, though, this is a documentation of my life. I close my eyes and picture each moment, the surrounding sounds, sights, smells, and feelings. Writing has become my coping mechanism through this journey. I've been so afraid of forgetting, of letting these memories blur and distort with time, that writing it all down has brought me comfort. I know I'm capturing these memories as they're happening, so my children and I can return to them when needed, to reflect, to rejoice, to mourn, and to feel confident in my progress. I haven't moved on yet. I don't know that anyone moves on from loss like this, but I am moving forward. I still cry myself to sleep some nights, I still sit in my closet clutching Brian's favorite sweatshirt and talk to him as if he were here, I still miss him, and miss our life together, I still look at our beautiful children who look just like him, each of them with a dimple in their left cheek and charismatic, kind spirits, and wish he could see how amazing they are. But I also laugh out loud now, I smile and take countless photos of all the adventures the kids and I go on, I celebrate the milestones we reach as a family, and I say with confidence that we're finding our way forward. I see how far I've come these last two years, and I know Brian would be so unbelievably proud of us. Knowing this pushes me to want more, to do more, and to not waste a single moment of my time here. If these two years have taught me anything, it's that we, as humans, are resilient creatures—if we allow ourselves to be. We can overcome and power through physical and emotional exhaustion, spirit depletion, and the worst experiences life could throw at us. We just have to want to. It's on us as individuals to put in the work and make it happen.

I wasn't sure how to end this book. I've written about the highest of highs and the lowest of lows we've experienced as a family these past two years, and just as I sat down to wrap up these stories and tell you how we're finding our way as a family of four—chaos erupted again. This time chaos not only affected our family, but our neighbors, our friends, our country, and the world. The words COVID-19 and Corona virus quickly changed from something we were reading and hearing about in the news to a part of our everyday vocabulary, the effects of which have changed our everyday lives. I type this out now with a cloth mask covering my nose and mouth, a bottle of hand sanitizer in my bag next to me, and the people and world around me in complete turmoil as we navigate a worldwide pandemic. We're living in an uncertain state right now. People are scared. Families, jobs, lifestyles, and ideas of what is, what was, and what will be, have all been shaken. This feeling of turmoil and uncertainty about the future isn't something a lot of people have had to experience before. It's scary, confusing, frustrating, and maddening at times, and these are feelings I understand. Izzy, Hudson, Addy, and I have lived through our world being turned upside down and have spent the last three years of our lives figuring out how to come together—regardless of the circumstances happening around us—to live our best lives. We've lived through uncertainty, through having more questions than answers, through falling asleep tonight worried for what tomorrow might bring. This isn't to say we as a family, and me, as a solo parent of three aren't scared or cautious about what's happening around us, but it is to say that I feel prepared for how we're going to manage that fear. We're going to recognize that we can't control what's happening around us, but we can control our attitudes and responses toward it. We can control ourselves as individuals and as a family. So, as a family, we're buckling down. Our travel plans have all been canceled, adventures we'd been looking forward to put on hold, school days amended, birthday parties held via Facetime and Zoom, and quick trips to the store put on hold while my Amazon account has seen a significant increase in activity. Just like all of you, we're not sure when any of this will end and we can get back to our normal way of life. But instead of feeling like victims, we're getting creative and finding new ways to spend our days. We're spending as much time as we can outdoors—hiking, swimming, playing at the river, and going for long drives. We're returning to the ocean, to celebrate Brian's life and his legacy, and to make new memories as a family. We're adapting and overcoming, and we're understanding that things are going to happen in our lives that we don't feel prepared for and that we don't know how to handle, but that the best way to get through it is to draw upon the lessons we've learned along the way and recognize how strong and resilient we each are. We will find a way through it.

I've heard countless times these last three years how lucky my children are to have me as their mom, but the truth is, I'm lucky to have them. Together, we've experienced the best and worst life has to offer, and there isn't anybody else out there I'd rather be on this adventure with. We're living life on our own terms, making it up as we go along, and finding what works for us—something I strongly encourage families around the globe do. This is our one life, our one chance, and we want to live a life we'll remember. We haven't made a bucket list, we aren't waiting for the right time to go after our goals.

We're instead choosing to experience life as it comes at us, taking advantage of every opportunity and living our best lives. We still have schoolwork to do, laundry to put away, squabbles between siblings to squash, errands to run, and I don't know what's next for us, or even what the world will look like a year from now. But I can tell you, I'm confident that Izzy, Hudson, Addy, and I will be able to say we spent this time making it count, and that our days will have been filled with love, laughter, and adventure.

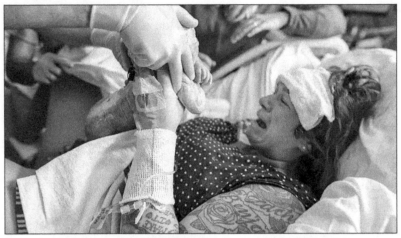

In a simultaneous moment of incredible joy and devastating sadness,
Adeline Makai Bugge is born and placed on my chest for the first time.

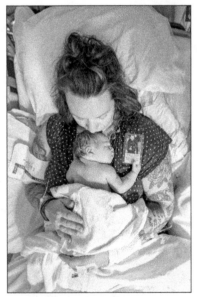

Addy takes hold of the only tangible
representation she'll ever have
of her dad; a photo taken of him
months before his death.

Santorini, Greece. Addy cheeses
at the camera while Brae films
for our family documentary.

Taking a moment to scatter some of Brian's ashes in Greystones, Ireland.

Izzy; age four. Looking through the window of a holding room at Auschwitz concentration camp.

Hudson being reunited with
Baby Bear after a tumultuous
night in Zermatt, Switzerland

The birthday cake heard 'round the world.
Izzy's fifth birthday with the melted cake
in St. Galen, Switzerland.

Hudson, age three, runs ahead to wrap his arms around this scuba diver statue in Oslo, Norway.

The Europe Crew.
From left to right:
Ashley (35)
Addy (11 months)
Kasey (32) Izzy (4)
Kayla (21) Hudson (3)

Forcing my way through a smile as Izzy and Hudson meet their new sister for the first time.
Still suicidal, I wasn't ready for this to be the reality of our family photos without Brian in them.

Year one memorial dive. my first time back in the water, I'm placing a flag on the stern of the Sea Tiger; the wreck Brian was attempting to dive when he died.

Six months pregnant and with my arm wrapped tightly around Brian's urn, I'm escorted outside to witness the three-volley salute at his military funeral.

Three adults. Three children. Three backpacks. Three car seats.
This was what we carried with us for two months through eight countries of Europe.

Izzy (4) comforting Addy (10 months) at their dad's gravesite where we had some of his ashes placed in Punchbowl National Cemetery. Honolulu, Hawaii.

Ashley and all three kids while waiting
for our early morning flight out of Athens, Greece.

Ashley and kids taking a moment to savor the journey they'd been on, and the moments which brought them here. Santorini, Greece.

Ashley and kids on Dalkey Island, Ireland.

Brian (35) Ashley (34) Izzy (3) Hudson (1) and baby Adeline in mom's belly. This is the last photo of the Bugge family to include Brian. Taken Mother's Day weekend 2018 at Turtle Bay Resort on the North Shore of Oahu. Brian would die exactly one week later.

Brian J Bugge 26 June 1982 – 20 May 2018.
Husband. Father. Diver. Sailor. Explorer.
The love of my life and the reason for this book.

Auntie Linda meets baby Adeline for the first time.

Commemorating an incredible few days spent in Malta with matching tattoos.

Ashley and dive team taking a moment to say 'A Hui Hou' to Brian
after placing his living reef memorial on the ocean floor. Honolulu, Hawaii.

Moving Day. A representative of the US Navy watches
over the arrival of our household goods. This was
the first time the kids and I would see our household
possessions since leaving Hawaii months prior.

Nikki and I. Brian's sister by family,
mine by choice.

Izzy and Mama enjoying a special moment
together. Zermatt, Switzerland.

About the Author

A shley Bugge is a widow-turned-author whose writing has been featured by Emmy nominated, *Whitney Reynolds* and whose story of turning tragedy into triumph will leave you feeling inspired to do the same. Ashley uses humor and personal tales of exploration, family and travel to share her story of love and eventual loss as she becomes a pregnant military widow at the age of thirty four.

Ashley currently resides in Washington State with her beautiful three children, Isabel, Hudson and Adeline. She's a master scuba diver, explorer, and water enthusiast who finds joy volunteering with her polar expedition team and sharing her love of the ocean with her children.

Ashley is the bestselling author of *Always Coming Back Home* which chronicles the love and loss of her beloved husband, Brian, as well as, 'A Hui Hou: Until We Meet Again' which she co-authored with her own three children to help young families through the grieving process of losing a loved one.

You can learn more about Ashley Bugge here:

www.ashleybugge.com

And please connect with Ashley Bugge here:
www.facebook.com/ashleybuggexo
www.instagram.com/ashley.bugge
info@ashleybugge.com

A free ebook edition is available with the purchase of this book.

To claim your free ebook edition:

1. Visit MorganJamesBOGO.com
2. Sign your name CLEARLY in the space
3. Complete the form and submit a photo of the entire copyright page
4. You or your friend can download the ebook to your preferred device

Morgan James BOGO™

A **FREE** ebook edition is available for you or a friend with the purchase of this print book.

CLEARLY SIGN YOUR NAME ABOVE

Instructions to claim your free ebook edition:
1. Visit MorganJamesBOGO.com
2. Sign your name CLEARLY in the space above
3. Complete the form and submit a photo of this entire page
4. You or your friend can download the ebook to your preferred device

Print & Digital Together Forever.

Snap a photo

Free ebook

Read anywhere

CPSIA information can be obtained
at www.ICGtesting.com
Printed in the USA
JSHW040640270822
29844JS00001B/7